"*United to Christ, Walking in the Spirit* c of Paul's short but majestic letter to th . union with Christ, the teaching about the church, and the call to walk well are all well handled. If you desire to understand the theme of this letter, this book is for you."

Darrell L. Bock, Executive Director of Cultural Engagement, The Hendricks Center, Dallas Theological Seminary

"Few books of the Bible lay out the height, depth, and breadth of the gospel like Ephesians. Benjamin Merkle puts the riches of this beloved Pauline epistle on full display, offering fresh insights into God's plan, union with Christ, life in the Spirit, the unity of the church, and spiritual warfare. Whether you are a pastor, teacher, small-group leader, or simply someone who wants to better understand Ephesians, this accessible book will deepen your love for Christ and show you how to live out the gospel more faithfully."

Matthew S. Harmon, Professor of New Testament Studies, Grace College and Theological Seminary; author, *Asking the Right Questions: A Practical Guide to Understanding and Applying the Bible*

"With strong exegetical support of his biblical theology, and with equally strong biblical theology considerations guiding his exegetical analysis, *United to Christ, Walking in the Spirit* is a gift to the body of Christ. In this small volume, Benjamin Merkle gives a masterful reading of Ephesians' argument and individual themes. He reads in concert with the best scholarship on Ephesians as he explains Paul's understanding of the role of the church in the decree of God—in redemptive history—and the treasures of the individual elements that are part of the web of our salvation. Anyone wishing to enjoy the book of Ephesians with greater depth and joy should have this work close at hand."

Eric C. Redmond, Professor of Bible, Moody Bible Institute

United to Christ, Walking in the Spirit

New Testament Theology

Edited by Thomas R. Schreiner and Brian S. Rosner

The Beginning of the Gospel: A Theology of Mark, Peter Orr

From the Manger to the Throne: A Theology of Luke, Benjamin L. Gladd

The Mission of the Triune God: A Theology of Acts, Patrick Schreiner

United to Christ, Walking in the Spirit: A Theology of Ephesians, Benjamin L. Merkle

The Joy of Hearing: A Theology of the Book of Revelation, Thomas R. Schreiner

United to Christ, Walking in the Spirit

A Theology of Ephesians

Benjamin L. Merkle

WHEATON, ILLINOIS

Library of Congress Cataloging-in-Publication Data

Names: Merkle, Benjamin L., 1971- author. | Schreiner, Thomas R., editor. | Rosner, Brian S., editor.
Title: United to Christ, walking in the Spirit : a theology of Ephesians / Benjamin L. Merkle ; Thomas R. Schreiner and Brian S. Rosner, editors.
Description: Wheaton, Illinois : Crossway, 2022. | Series: New Testament theology | Includes bibliographical references and index.
Identifiers: LCCN 2021056702 (print) | LCCN 2021056703 (ebook) | ISBN 9781433573699 (trade paperback) | ISBN 9781433573705 (pdf) | ISBN 9781433573712 (mobipocket) | ISBN 9781433573729 (epub)
Subjects: LCSH: Bible. Ephesians—Theology.
Classification: LCC BS2695.52 .M475 2022 (print) | LCC BS2695.52 (ebook) | DDC 227/.506—dc23/eng/20220126
LC record available at https://lccn.loc.gov/2021056702
LC ebook record available at https://lccn.loc.gov/2021056703

Contents

Series Preface

THERE ARE REMARKABLY FEW TREATMENTS of the big ideas of single books of the New Testament. Readers can find brief coverage in Bible dictionaries, in some commentaries, and in New Testament theologies, but such books are filled with other information and are not devoted to unpacking the theology of each New Testament book in its own right. Technical works concentrating on various themes of New Testament theology often have a narrow focus, treating some aspect of the teaching of, say, Matthew or Hebrews in isolation from the rest of the book's theology.

The New Testament Theology series seeks to fill this gap by providing students of Scripture with readable book-length treatments of the distinctive teaching of each New Testament book or collection of books. The volumes approach the text from the perspective of biblical theology. They pay due attention to the historical and literary dimensions of the text, but their main focus is on presenting the teaching of particular New Testament books about God and his relations to the world on their own terms, maintaining sight of the Bible's overarching narrative and Christocentric focus. Such biblical theology is of fundamental importance to biblical and expository preaching and informs exegesis, systematic theology, and Christian ethics.

The twenty volumes in the series supply comprehensive, scholarly, and accessible treatments of theological themes from an evangelical perspective. We envision them being of value to students, preachers, and interested laypeople. When preparing an expository sermon series, for example, pastors can find a healthy supply of informative commentaries, but there are few options for coming to terms with the overall teaching of each book of the New Testament. As well as being useful in sermon and Bible study preparation, the volumes will also be of value as textbooks in college and seminary exegesis classes. Our prayer is that they contribute to a deeper understanding of and commitment to the kingdom and glory of God in Christ.

Ephesians is deeply theological and meditative, reflecting on the great salvation that is ours in Christ Jesus. Paul doesn't dispute with opponents as he does in many of his letters. Instead he composes a letter that is profoundly theological and at the same time wonderfully practical. One of the striking features of the letter is the central place of the church in God's plan, steering us away from the individualism and fierce independence that is characteristic of many in our days. Ben Merkle is an expert and faithful interpreter of one of the most important Pauline letters, leading us to explore all the riches that belong to us in Christ Jesus our Lord. He mines the letter both theologically and practically, showing us that redemptive history centers on and points to Jesus the Christ.

Thomas R. Schreiner and Brian S. Rosner

Abbreviations

AB	Anchor Bible
Ant.	Josephus, *Antiquities*
BDAG	*Greek-English Lexicon of the New Testament and Other Early Christian Literature, 3rd ed.*
BECNT	Baker Exegetical Commentary on the New Testament
BHGNT	Baylor Handbook on the Greek New Testament
DPL	*Dictionary of Paul and His Letters*
EEC	Evangelical Exegetical Commentary
ICC	International Critical Commentary
JETS	*Journal of the Evangelical Theological Society*
J.W.	*Jewish Wars*
L&N	*Greek-English Lexicon of the New Testament Based on Semantic Domains*
NICNT	New International Commentary on the New Testament
NIVAC	NIV Application Commentary
PNTC	Pillar New Testament Commentary
WBC	Word Biblical Commentary
ZECNT	Zondervan Exegetical Commentary on the New Testament

Introduction

FOR ITS SIZE (SIX CHAPTERS AND 155 VERSES), Paul's letter to the Ephesians has had a profound impact on the life and theology of the church.[1] Klyne Snodgrass asserts, "Only the Psalms, the Gospel of John, and Romans have been as significant as Ephesians in shaping the life and thought of Christians."[2] Harold Hoehner likewise declares, "The Letter to the Ephesians is one of the most influential documents in the Christian church."[3] This influence is due to the robust and diverse nature of the theology embedded in this short epistle. Paul addresses topics such as God's sovereignty, the nature of salvation, race relations, roles in marriage and the family, the unity of the church, and spiritual warfare.

The apostle Paul wrote this letter to the Christians living in (or near) Ephesus to instruct them in the faith and encourage them in their behavior. Along with Philippians, Colossians, and Philemon, Ephesians is known as one of the "Prison Epistles" since it was written during a two-year imprisonment in Rome (AD 60–62).[4] Paul writes primarily,

1   See Rudolf Schnackenburg, "The Influence of the Epistle throughout History," in *Ephesians: A Commentary* (Edinburgh: T&T Clark, 1991), 311–42.
2   Klyne Snodgrass, *Ephesians*, NIVAC (Grand Rapids, MI: Zondervan, 1996), 17. Similarly, Raymond Brown declares, "Among the Pauline writings only Rom[ans] can match Eph[esians] as a candidate for exercising the most influence on Christian thought and spirituality." *An Introduction to the New Testament* (New York: Doubleday, 1997), 620.
3   Harold W. Hoehner, *Ephesians: An Exegetical Commentary* (Grand Rapids, MI: Baker, 2002), 1. Markus Barth writes, "Ephesians is among the greatest letters under the name of the apostle Paul." *Ephesians 1–3*, AB 34 (Garden City, NY: Doubleday, 1974), 3.
4   See Eph. 1:1; 3:1; 4:1; 6:20. Other possible options for the date and location of Paul's imprisonment include sometime during his three-year visit to Ephesus (AD 52–56) or during his imprisonment in Caesarea (AD 57–59).

though not exclusively, to Gentile Christians (2:11–12; 3:1; 4:17), providing first a theological foundation (1:1–3:21) and then instructing them how to live (4:1–6:20).

This book, *United to Christ, Walking in the Spirit*, has five chapters that are based on prominent theological features of the book of Ephesians: (1) the plan of *God*; (2) union with *Christ*; (3) walking according to the *Spirit*; (4) the unity of the *church*; and (5) spiritual warfare in the *present age*. Although many of these topics overlap with major loci in systematic theology (e.g., theology, Christology, pneumatology, ecclesiology, and eschatology), these topics are nuanced so as to be particular to Ephesians. Chapter 1, "The Plan of God," first delves into the meaning of Paul's statement that it is God's plan "to unite all things in him [i.e., Christ], things in heaven and things on earth" (1:10). It also discusses God's plan in salvation (including election, redemption, adoption/inheritance, perseverance, and regeneration), God's plan for the apostle Paul (including his calling and his receiving the mystery), and God's plan in prayer (including Paul's two prayers and his exhortation to pray and request for prayer). Chapter 2 is an in-depth study on the doctrine of union with Christ in Ephesians. In particular, using Constantine Campbell's work as a foundation, it explicates the four concepts of union, participation, identification, and incorporation. Chapter 3, "Walking according to the Spirit," contains three emphases, with the final emphasis receiving the most attention. First, I discuss the former way of walking, which involved being dead in sin, living as alienated strangers, and possessing futile minds and hardened hearts. Second, I explain how the foundation of walking in the Spirit is based on God's work in Christ for us. Finally, I give attention to the freedom of walking in the Spirit, which means walking in good works, walking worthy of our calling, walking according to the new self, walking in love, walking as children of light, walking with wisdom, walking filled by the Spirit, and walking faithfully with the family of God. Chapter 4 focuses on the unity of the church, the body of Christ. Because of their mutual relationship with Christ, Jews and Gentiles can live in peace with one another. But the unity of the church allows room for a diversity of gifts that leads to the maturity of the body. Chapter 5, "Spiritual Warfare in the Present Age," explains the present rule of Satan (his kingdom, his minions, and his power and influence), the present battle (the believer's struggle, strength, and stand), and finally the meaning and eschatological tension between the present age and the age to come.

The goal of this book is to offer an accessible summary of the theology of Ephesians that highlights the work of God through his Son for the believer who is then able to love and enjoy God because of the ongoing work of the Spirit. It is *because* believers are united to Christ that they *can* walk in the Spirit. Paul has much to say about the behavior of Christians, but such behavior is always based on first beholding and believing in the promises of God that are given to us through Christ. We love because he first loved us, and we serve because he first served us.

1

The Plan of God

IF *THEOLOGY* IS THE STUDY OF GOD, then it is appropriate that we begin our theology with God and his eternal plan. After all, Paul informs us that God is the one who works "all things according to the counsel of his will" (Eph. 1:11). As the Creator of all things (3:9), God is the sovereign and benevolent King who is orchestrating his grand plan to redeem humanity through the seed of a woman (Gen. 3:15). The rebellion of angels and humanity alienated them from their Creator and, in the case of humanity, from one another. What began in the garden with the fall of Adam and Eve culminates with the Son of God, Jesus Christ, being first lifted up on a cross and then lifted up to the Father's side in glory. Specifically in Ephesians, we will consider (1) God's plan to unite all things in Christ, (2) God's plan in salvation, (3) God's plan in calling the apostle Paul, and (4) God's plan in prayer.

God's Plan to Unite All Things in Christ

In Ephesians 1:9–10, Paul provides us with a central statement of his letter. In fact, these verses (especially 1:10) represent the high point of the eulogy (a prolonged blessing) found in 1:3–14.[1] Paul indicates that God's "plan" is "to unite all things in [Christ], things in heaven

---

1 S. M. Baugh suggests that 1:9–10 "contain one of the central statements of the opening benediction and of the epistle as a whole" (*Ephesians*, EEC [Bellingham, WA: Lexham, 2016], 92). Frank Thielman states that 1:10 "is the chief theological concern of the letter's

and things on earth." The term translated "plan" (*oikonomia*) can mean (1) the act of administrating, (2) that which is administered (i.e., a plan), or (3) the office or role of an administrator.[2] The context suggests that here it refers to God's act of administrating his plan of redemption. The repeated vocabulary of the opening fourteen verses also indicates that God's plan is central. Paul mentions God's "will" (*thelēma*; 1:1, 5, 9, 11), "purpose" or "good pleasure" (*eudokia*; 1:5, 9), "purpose" (*prothesis*; 1:11), and "counsel" (*boulē*; 1:11), as well as verbs such as "choose" (*eklegō*; 1:4) and "predestine" (*prooridzō*; 1:5, 11).

But what does it mean that God's plan is to unite all things in Christ? There are several truths related to this statement that should be highlighted. First, God desired to *reveal* his plan to his people. He lavished his grace on us by "making known to us the mystery of his will" (1:9). Thus God is to be blessed and praised precisely because he graciously revealed his plan to redeem fallen humanity. This plan was not something God's people could calculate or deduce by their own reasoning, but it displays the overwhelming grace of God. So Paul writes to inform his readers of God's gracious purpose and to instruct them of their place in his eternal plan.

Second, this plan is the revealing of a *mystery*. What was previously concealed as to the exact nature of God's plan of redemption through Christ is now revealed. Although the Old Testament prophets progressively unfolded the divine design, the precise details were often shrouded and seen as shadows behind a veil. God designed all along that his people understand his purposes, but many of the details of this plan were not disclosed to his people. Although the Old Testament included the nations being blessed, it was not clear that Gentiles would be considered equal with Israel. But now, in the gospel God has revealed the mystery of his plan, which has the ultimate goal of unit-

---

first main section (1:3–3:21)" (*Theology of the New Testament: A Canonical and Synthetic Approach* [Grand Rapids, MI: Zondervan, 2010], 395).

2   *Oikonomia* occurs eight other times in the New Testament (Luke 16:2, 3, 4; 1 Cor. 9:17; Eph. 3:2, 9; Col. 1:25; 1 Tim. 1:4) and has been translated in a number of ways in this verse: (1) "administration" (CSB, NASB), (2) "plan" (NRSV), and (3) "dispensation" (KJV, NKJV).

ing all things in Christ. More specifically, it involves uniting Jews and Gentiles into the one, new people of God. Thus the term *mystery* in Paul refers to something that was hidden but is now revealed, especially as it relates to God's plan to include the Gentiles into the people of God.[3] In Ephesians the mystery involves the all-inclusive plan of God to unite all things (including Jews and Gentiles) into the one body of Christ.

Third, this plan was revealed by God "according to his purpose" (1:9). The word translated "purpose" is often rendered "good pleasure." The goodness and love of God are manifested in his plan for humankind. Because God delights in redeeming lost sinners, that is what he purposed to do. So just as God predestined his people for adoption according to his good pleasure (1:5), he also has disclosed his plans to them for his good pleasure.

Fourth, God set forth his plan "in Christ" (1:9). That is, God did not conceive of this plan in isolation, but Christ was intimately involved in planning our redemption with the Father. As Arnold notes, "Christ was not a passive observer of all that the Father was doing, but participated with him in the delight of planning a way to overcome the obstacle that sin presented to the divine-human relationship."[4] Just as God chose and adopted his people in Christ (1:5), so too God's plan to reveal the mystery of his purposes is rooted in and revolves around Christ.

Fifth, God set forth this plan "for the fullness of time" (1:10). From the beginning God had a plan of redemption that was revealed in bits and pieces through the Old Testament prophets but was hidden until the coming of the Messiah. The exact phrase "fullness of time" does not occur elsewhere in the Bible, but the closest parallel to this unique construction is found in Galatians 4:4, where Paul states, "But when the fullness of time had come, God sent forth his Son, born of woman, born under the law."[5] The incarnation, ministry, life, death,

---

3   See Rom. 11:25; 16:25–27; Eph. 3:3, 4, 9; Col. 1:26–27; and 1 Tim. 3:16. Paul uses the term *mystery* (*mystērion*) twenty-one times, including six times in Ephesians (1:9; 3:3, 4, 9; 5:32; 6:19).

4   Clinton E. Arnold, *Ephesians*, ZECNT (Grand Rapids, MI: Zondervan, 2010), 87.

5   Although the English translations are the same, the Greek contains two different words for "time." Gal. 4:4 has *chronos*, whereas Eph. 1:10 has *kairos* (cf. Dan. 2:19–22).

resurrection, and ascension of Jesus comprise the pivotal act in redemptive history.

Sixth, God's perfect plan is "to unite all things" (Eph. 1:10) through his Son.[6] This phrase describes the content of the mystery that was hidden in the past but is now revealed in the gospel. The only other New Testament use of the verb *to unite* is in Romans 13:9 where Paul notes that all of the Old Testament commandments can be "summed up" by the command to love your neighbor as yourself. "All things" most likely refers to the entire universe (cf. Eph. 3:9). This meaning is confirmed when Paul amplifies this thought by adding, "things in heaven and things on earth" (1:10). That is, it refers to not just all humanity but also the angelic realm, both good and evil, and the entire cosmos. Paul writes elsewhere that through Christ, God will "reconcile to himself all things, whether on earth or in heaven, making peace by the blood of his cross" (Col. 1:20). In Romans he declares that creation itself is longing for its own redemption (Rom. 8:18–22). Thus God is in the process of uniting the entire universe around Christ. This uniting includes both the heavenly and earthly dimensions. God's plan is unequivocally Christocentric.

Seventh, this plan *centers on Christ*. That is, the triune God's work of redemption hinges on the incarnate Son of God—Jesus, the Messiah.[7] Baugh comments, "The work of Christ on the cross is the central axis for the history of all creation."[8] God's purpose is to unite all things "in him [Christ]" (Eph. 1:10). Christ is not only the means by which God will unite all the disparate elements of creation together; he is the center and focal point through whom and for whom all this will take place. Jesus defeated sin and death through his resurrection and ascension and is seated at God's right hand ruling sovereignly over his creation.

6   The verb "to unite" is variously translated in English as "to bring together" (CSB), "summing up" (NASB), "to bring unity to" (NIV), "gather together" (NKJV), and "to gather up" (NRSV).

7   In 1:1–14 the name or title "Christ" is explicitly or implicitly mentioned (usually through a pronoun) at least fifteen times, and the phrases "in Christ" (*en Christō*), "in him" (*en autō*), "in whom" (*en hō*), or "in the beloved" (*en tō ēgapēmenō*) occur eleven times.

8   Baugh, *Ephesians*, 93.

He has defeated all powers, with all his foes vanquished under his feet (1:20–22). Furthermore, Christ is head of the church, his body, which is comprised of people from diverse ethnic groups but who have all submitted to follow the Lamb of God (1:22–23). He is the one who abolished the law "that he might create in himself one new man in place of the two" (2:15). Thus "all things" will be brought under Christ's lordship, whether the vanquished or the victorious. As Paul writes in Philippians, "At the name of Jesus every knee should bow, in heaven and on earth and under the earth, and every tongue confess that Jesus Christ is Lord, to the glory of God the Father" (Phil. 2:10–11). Thus "God achieves his purpose for all things through what he accomplished in one person, Christ."[9] God's gracious purpose to restore harmony for the universe centers on Jesus. In Christ, the final, climactic phase has begun in uniting all things and in bringing God's plan to fulfillment.

God's Plan in Salvation

The ultimate goal of God's plan includes the redemption of the entire cosmos (Eph. 1:10) and is therefore not limited to humanity. But the renewal of humanity is the key component of God's cosmic plan to unite all things in Christ. God's plan to save his people is featured prominently in the first two chapters of Ephesians, especially 1:3–14. In the original Greek, this passage consists of one long sentence of 202 words. These verses contain an extended praise to God for his blessings that believers receive from their union with Christ; namely, God's election, redemption, inheritance, and perseverance. The topic of God's amazing love in regeneration is highlighted in 2:4–10.

Election

As Paul begins his letter in a typical Old Testament or Jewish style of a prolonged blessing (eulogy), he urges his readers to bless God since he has blessed us "with every spiritual blessing" (1:3). Specifically, the focus is on *spiritual* blessings or blessings that pertain to life in the Spirit. The

9 Andrew D. Lincoln, *Ephesians*, WBC 42 (Dallas: Word, 1990), 34.

first reason Paul gives for believers to praise God is his divine election. That is, God is worthy of our praise precisely *because* he has chosen us in Christ before the foundation of the world.

THE MEANING OF ELECTION

Election is God's choice of individuals to receive his favor before they have done anything good or bad (Rom. 9:10–11). It is not a choice that is based on (or in light of) certain deeds or choices that we make but is based solely on God's sovereign grace (Rom. 9:16). Here in Ephesians, Paul uses two different verbs to convey this idea. He writes that God "chose" (*eklegomai*, 1:4) and "predestined" (*prooridzō*, 1:5, 11) those who believe and follow Christ. More specifically, Paul states that God's choice of his people is related to them being predestined to be a part of his family ("for adoption," 1:5). Thus Paul is stressing that believers should praise God because he predestined them and chose them to be his children and receive all the benefits that such a privilege affords. The verb *predestine* can also be translated "predetermine" or "foreordain" and occurs only four other times in the New Testament (Acts 4:28; Rom. 8:29, 30; 1 Cor. 2:7). In every occurrence it refers to the work of God that emphasizes God's sole initiative in election or predestination.

THE CAUSE OF ELECTION

Election is the divine choice of God to grant eternal life to undeserving sinners based solely on his love and not on the goodness of those receiving his grace. It is not arbitrary but part of his grand plan of salvation and grounded in his eternal wisdom. Paul indicates that God elected or predestined his people "in love."[10] That God sovereignly elects a people for himself is not original to Paul but is a theme that runs throughout the Bible. In the Old Testament, God graciously chose Abraham and blessed him to become a blessing to the nations (Gen. 12:1–3). Later,

---

10 Although it is possible that "in love" modifies what precedes ("holy and blameless before him in love," NKJV, NRSV), it is more likely that it modifies what follows ("In love he predestined us," ESV, CSB, NASB, NIV) since the focus of the eulogy is on God's work of blessing his people.

God chose the nation of Israel to be his treasured possession, not because they were greater than the other nations or because of their righteousness, but because of his love (Deut. 7:6–8; 14:2). Similarly, in Christ, God chose individuals from all the peoples of the world to become his people, a decision based on his amazing love.

Paul also indicates that God's election is rooted in the work of Christ. Four times in Ephesians 1:3–6 he links the blessings of God's sovereign, electing grace to the Son: we are blessed "in Christ" (1:3); we are chosen "in him" (1:4); we are adopted "through Jesus Christ" (1:5); and we are blessed because of being "in the Beloved" (1:5). The blessings we receive are reserved specifically for those who are united with Christ through faith, those who trust in his death, resurrection, and ascension. The ability to call God our Father is possible only through Christ, who alone provides access to the Father because of Christ's finished work on the cross. Christ is not only the recipient *par excellence* of the Father's love and affection (Col. 1:13), but it is through his beloved Son that we receive his blessings. Furthermore, God's work of predestination was done "according to the purpose of his will" (Eph. 1:5). The basis of God's choice was his own will carried out in accordance with his "purpose," or "good pleasure," indicating that the choosing of his people was something in which God delighted. God's choice was also done in accordance with his "will." God has a definite plan and redemptive purpose for adopting wayward sinners into his family.

THE TIME OF ELECTION

Interestingly, Paul indicates that the time of believers' election was "before the foundation of the world" (1:4). This phrase also occurs in John 17:24 (referring to the Father's love of the Son "before the foundation of the world") and 1 Peter 1:20 ("[Christ] was foreknown before the foundation of the world but was made manifest in the last times for the sake of you"). Here in Ephesians, God's choice in election occurred before time and creation. God's timing emphasizes that this choice was based on God's sovereign purpose and not human merit. Paul declares in Romans 9 that God selected Jacob over Esau "though [the twins] were not yet born and had done nothing either good or bad—in order that God's purpose of election might continue, not because of works but because of him who calls" (Rom. 9:11).

THE PURPOSE OF ELECTION

God's electing love and grace have a purpose. Paul writes that God chose us so "that we should be holy and blameless before him" (Eph. 1:4; cf. Col. 1:22). Those who have the privilege of being elected to receive God's grace have the responsibility of living according to God's word. Redemption has a divine purpose and intended result. God desires not only to forgive our sins but also to conform us to the image of his beloved Son (Rom. 8:29–30). When God chose his people, they were *not* holy and blameless. They deserved his judgment and wrath. Because of his great love and electing grace, he chose us, and through the power of the indwelling Holy Spirit, is transforming the thoughts and actions of his people. Ultimately, all of God's purpose in election is done "to the praise of his glorious grace" (Eph. 1:6). This refrain is also later echoed in 1:12 and 14 ("to the praise of his glory"), demonstrating that God's purpose is to make his name great through his great mercy that he bestows on undeserving sinners.

Redemption

THE MEANING OF REDEMPTION

The term *redemption* (*apolutrōsis*) indicates release or liberation from imprisonment or captivity.[11] Redemption is a concept not only known in the Greco-Roman society; it is also found in the Old Testament where it describes both the release of slaves from bondage (Ex. 21:8; Lev. 25:48) and the deliverance of God's people from slavery in Egypt (Deut. 7:8; 9:26; 13:5; 1 Chron. 17:21). Elsewhere Paul writes that believers have been "bought with a price" (1 Cor. 6:20; 7:23) and that "Christ redeemed us from the curse of the law by becoming a curse for us" (Gal. 3:13).

---

11 The term *redemption* (*apolutrōsis*) occurs nine times in the New Testament, with seven references found in Paul's writings (Rom. 3:24; 8:23; 1 Cor. 1:30; Eph. 1:7, 14; 4:30; Col. 1:14; cf. Heb. 9:15; 11:35).

Paul expresses that believers should not only praise God for his election, but also bless him for his redemption: "In him we have redemption" (Eph. 1:7). Paul transitions from God's predetermining choice before time, to his work of redemption in the course of history. Just as God chose his people *in Christ*, so also they are redeemed "in him." This redemption is not simply a future hope (cf. 1:14) but is also a present reality ("*we have* redemption"). That is, believers now have the full hope of redemption, as well as its firstfruits, even though fullness of redemption awaits the new heavens and the new earth.

The redemption believers receive is clarified as "the forgiveness of our trespasses" (1:7). Forgiveness implies an offense that requires a just punishment. Here, Paul uses *trespasses* instead of the more common word *sins*, though the parallel passage in Colossians 1:14 uses the word *sins*. Paul later uses both concepts together: "you were dead in the trespasses and sins" (Eph. 2:1).[12]

THE MEANS OF REDEMPTION

In Ephesians 1:7 Paul specifically states that our redemption in Christ is "through his blood." That is, the blood of Christ is the *means* by which redemption is procured, with "blood" functioning as a metonymy (one word used for another word closely associated with it) for the sacrificial death of Jesus. Thus our deliverance comes only at the great price of Christ's death on the cross. Salvation is free simply because it has been paid for by another. It is free to us, but the cost was incalculable. This redemption that God initiated is "according to the riches of his grace" (1:7; see also 1:18; 3:8, 16; cf. Col. 1:27; 2:2–3). According to Ephesians 1:8, God *lavished* this grace upon his people, demonstrating the extent of his grace. Furthermore, God bestows this lavish grace on those in Christ "in all wisdom and insight,"[13] demonstrating that it is all part

---

12 The concept of forgiveness of sins is found in Mark 1:4; Acts 2:38; 5:31; 10:43; 13:38; 26:18.

13 Although it is possible to take the phrase "in all wisdom and insight" with what follows in 1:9 (NASB, NIV, NRSV), it is best to take the phrase with what precedes (CSB, ESV, KJV, NKJV) for the following reasons: (1) Its similarity with the Greek of 1:6 and some of Paul's other statements (see Eph. 1:17–18; Col. 1:9). (2) In 1:3–14 most of the prepositional phrases occur after the verbs they modify.

of his well-designed and -executed plan. God's decision to lavish his kindness and favor upon them by securing the price of their redemption through the death of his beloved Son was in accordance with his infinite wisdom and insight.

In two passages redemption is linked to the Spirit, where Paul shifts from focusing on redemption that believers now possess to the future inheritance that they will receive. In chapter 1 Paul states that believers are "sealed with the promised Holy Spirit, who is the guarantee of our inheritance until we acquire possession of it" (1:13–14), and in chapter 4 he likewise asserts it is by the Holy Spirit that we are "sealed for the day of redemption" (4:30). Both of these passages are in the context of believers receiving a future inheritance that will undoubtedly be obtained because the Holy Spirit will ensure that God will complete his work of salvation (Phil. 1:6). Although it is not articulated, the inheritance that believers will receive includes the blessing of eternal fellowship with God (Pss. 16:5; 119:57; Lam. 3:24), a blessing that believers can now begin to enjoy. The "redemption" here is thus forward-oriented, looking to the completion of that redemption in the future. The "day of redemption" (Eph. 4:30) refers to the final day of salvation (or judgment) and most likely is referring to the same time as "the day of the Lord."[14]

Inheritance (Adoption)

In Ephesians 1:11–12 Paul supplies a third reason why believers should bless or praise God: he has given his people an inheritance based on their adoption (1:5). In the ESV, the verb translated "we have obtained an inheritance" (*klēroō*) could also be understood as "appoint by lot."[15] Based on the latter meaning, some have interpreted the text to mean that believers have been allotted to God as his inheritance or portion. If this interpretation is correct, then the passage does not refer to believers *receiving* an inheritance, but to the fact that believers *are* the

---

14 See 1 Cor. 1:8; 5:5; 2 Cor. 1:14; Phil. 1:6, 10; 2:16; 1 Thess. 5:2; 2 Thess. 2:2; 2 Pet. 3:10.
15 BDAG 549. The verb *klēroō* occurs only here in the New Testament, though it does occur three times in the Old Testament (1 Sam. 14:41; Isa. 17:11 [2x]).

inheritance that God obtains. Although the concept of God possessing his people as an inheritance is found in the Old Testament,[16] this interpretation is not consistent with the focus of the passage, which emphasizes the necessity for believers to praise God because of the blessings his people receive.[17] This theme is not only found in 1:11–12 but is also mentioned in 1:5, 14, 18 and 5:5.

THE REALITY OF THE INHERITANCE

Because of his great love, God has promised his people an inheritance (*klēronomia*). Although Paul does not go into detail as to the nature of the inheritance in Ephesians, in Galatians he connects it to the promise given to Abraham (Gal. 3:18). In the Old Testament, the concept of inheritance was often linked to the land promise that God gave to Abraham (Gen. 15:3–5; 17:8; 22:17; 28:4). And yet the promised inheritance cannot be limited to the land of Canaan, a truth found in the Old Testament (Pss. 22:27–28; 47:7–9; 72:8–11; Zeph. 3:9–10) and New Testament (Rom. 4:13). Thus inheritance consists of a renewed and transformed universe that is now promised but will be received only after Jesus returns. It is also likely, as Moo notes, that "the land becomes a tangible symbol of all that God promises to do for his people."[18]

Paul makes it clear that this "glorious inheritance" (Eph. 1:18) is something that awaits believers. Although the promise of this inheritance has been made (1:11), the reality of it is eschatological. Believers have been given the Holy Spirit, who is "the guarantee of our inheritance until we acquire possession of it, to the praise of his glory" (1:14). Now we are given the Holy Spirit, but in the future we will also

---

16   See Deut. 4:20; 9:29; 32:8–9; 1 Kings 8:51; Pss. 33:12; 106:40.

17   For example, in 1:14 Paul states that those who believed the gospel were sealed with the Holy Spirit, "who is the guarantee of our inheritance until we acquire possession of it." In Col. 1:12 Paul similarly prays that his readers would give thanks to God who qualified them "to share in the inheritance of the saints" (the Greek word here is *klēros*, which refers to one's lot or portion).

18   Douglas J. Moo, *The Letter to the Colossians and to Philemon*, PNTC (Grand Rapids, MI: Eerdmans, 2008), 312. See 1 Cor. 6:9–10; 15:50; Gal. 5:21; Heb. 1:14; 1 Pet. 1:4.

be given an inheritance. In 1:18 saints have been given the *hope* of a future inheritance, and in Colossians Paul uses the future tense in relation to this promised reward: "You will receive the inheritance as your reward" (Col. 3:24).

THE REASON FOR THE INHERITANCE

Believers will receive an inheritance because God has predestined them to receive this free gift, which is done in accordance with the purpose of his will. God does not simply elect his people with no purpose, but God's divine purpose of predestination is specifically that those chosen are adopted into his family as a free gift through the completed work of Christ (Eph. 1:5, 11). In the Old Testament, the nation of Israel was given the special privilege of being God's son. At the time of the exodus, God calls Israel "my firstborn son" (Ex. 4:22), and later God reminds his people through the prophet Hosea: "When Israel was a child, I loved him, and out of Egypt I called my son" (Hos. 11:1). Paul indicates that the privilege of adoption was one of the benefits graciously given to Israel (Rom. 9:4). Adoption was common in Greco-Roman culture, and those adopted were given the full status of the family and became heirs of the family's estate. Paul now applies this concept to believers (cf. Rom. 9:26; 2 Cor. 6:18).[19] Believers receive an inheritance because God has adopted them into his family to be coheirs with Christ.

The reason for believers obtaining an inheritance ultimately relates to God working out his purpose in history. Three times in the span of ten verses, Paul reminds his readers that God adopts and grants an inheritance to his people "according to the purpose of his will" (Eph. 1:5), "according to the purpose of him who works all things according to the counsel of his will" (1:11), and "to the praise of his glory" (1:14). God's choosing, saving, and blessing his people is all part of God's carefully considered and executed plan.

---

19 The term *adoption* (*huiothesia*) is used only five times in the New Testament, and only by Paul (Rom. 8:15, 23; 9:4; Gal. 4:5; Eph. 1:5; cf. Eph. 1:11, 14).

THE RECIPIENTS OF THE INHERITANCE

But who precisely are those who will receive the inheritance? It is those who are in Christ and those who walk according to his word. First, Paul makes it abundantly clear that union with Christ is the defining feature of the redeemed who await an inheritance. He declares that their adoption as sons is "through Jesus Christ" (1:5) and that it is "in him" that believers obtain an inheritance (1:11). Thus Paul emphasizes that it is through our union with Christ that believers are incorporated into the family of God and have become heirs to the blessings and promises made by the Father (cf. Rom. 8:17; Gal. 3:29; 4:1, 5, 7).

Second, Paul later clarifies that "everyone who is sexually immoral or impure, or who is covetous (that is, an idolater), has no inheritance in the kingdom of Christ and God" (Eph. 5:5).[20] Although Paul only mentions three groups, it is not limited to those specifically named. Rather, the point is that those who abandon the word of God and live immorally are not in Christ and therefore will not partake of the blessings that Christ has secured. Paul is not proclaiming that all those who commit such sins are necessarily excluded from God's heavenly kingdom but those who are characterized by such a lifestyle. It is those outside of Christ who live in persistent and unrepentant sin who have no future inheritance in the kingdom.

Perseverance

In 1:13 Paul provides the final reason for why believers should praise God: he has sealed them with the Holy Spirit. God ensures that his promises for his people are not in jeopardy. That is, he chooses them and adopts them into his family, he redeems them by the blood of Christ, and he provides them a glorious inheritance. But what if they fall away or permanently reject Christ? According to Paul, this will not happen since the Holy Spirit not only indwells his people but is the

20 Rosner defines the greedy (or covetous) as "those with a strong desire to acquire for themselves more and more money and possessions, because they love, trust, and obey wealth rather than God." Brian S. Rosner, *Greed as Idolatry: The Origin and Meaning of a Pauline Metaphor* (Grand Rapids, MI: Eerdmans, 2007), 129.

means by which they are sealed so as to guarantee that believers will receive their promised inheritance.

THE SEALING OF THE SPIRIT

Paul explains that when people hear and believe the truth of the gospel, they are immediately sealed with the Holy Spirit (1:13). He later adds that this sealing is not temporary but will endure until "the day of redemption" (4:30). Thus the Holy Spirit is the means by which God seals his people, which provides several benefits to believers. First, being sealed secures salvation, protecting someone from God's future wrath and judgment that will be poured out on the wicked. Second, because the Spirit serves as a deposit or down-payment, being sealed guarantees that believers will acquire their future inheritance. That is, the indwelling of the Spirit provides the assurance or guarantee that God's people will receive everything that God has promised and that Christ accomplished for them. The idea of being "sealed" also can signify identification of ownership (cf. 2 Cor. 1:22). Consequently, God is to be praised because he seals those who hear and believe the gospel, thereby claiming them as his own and securing their eschatological inheritance.

THE GUARANTEE OF THE SPIRIT

Believers will persevere in their faith until the end because they are sealed with the Spirit who thus is the "guarantee" that they will receive their promised inheritance (Eph. 1:14). The term *guarantee* (*arrabōn*) is used only three times in the New Testament, all by Paul and all referring to the Holy Spirit (2 Cor. 1:22; 5:5; cf. Rom. 8:23). In the Greco-Roman world, a guarantee functioned as a down-payment that signified the expectation that the full amount would be given once the terms of service had been met. As a result, the guarantee was a promise of more to come. Likewise, God has granted the Holy Spirit to his people with the assurance and expectation of the future inheritance (cf. 2 Cor. 5:5). Paul therefore declares that the presence of God's Spirit will continue "until we acquire possession of [our inheritance]" (Eph. 1:14). Later, Paul indicates that believers have been sealed "for the day of redemption" (4:30), which refers to the day of salvation (for believers) or the day of judgment (for unbelievers). There is no doubt that believers will persevere until the end because the indwelling presence of the Spirit seals believers and guarantees that they will receive their inheritance.

Regeneration

In Ephesians 2:1–3 Paul offers a bleak view of humanity: all people are dead in their sins and deserve God's wrath. Beginning in 2:4, however, Paul introduces the good news of the gospel into our hopeless condition: because of his great love, mercy, and grace, God intervened and brought life into our dead, hardened hearts. The essence of this passage is that we were dead, but God makes us alive. Regeneration is thus the free and sovereign work of God, who takes sinners who are spiritually dead and makes them alive through the work of the Spirit.

THE WORK OF REGENERATION

Humanity's desperate situation is contrasted by two key words: "But God" (2:4). Without God's intervening grace, God's unending wrath would have been our destiny since we were guilty of offending God by walking in our "trespasses and sins" (2:1) and following the ways of the world, the flesh, and the devil. Paul uses three verbs to describe the regenerating and salvific work of God—and all three of these terms underscore the believer's union with Christ: "God . . . made us alive together with [*synezōopoiēsen*] Christ . . . and raised us up with [*synēgeiren*] him and seated us with [*synekathisen*] him" (2:4–6). Each of these verbs in Greek is a compound verb that includes a prepositional prefix (*syn-*) meaning "together with." The threefold blessing of regeneration, exaltation, and coronation that was first accomplished by God in Christ is what believers partake in. Although Christ's resurrection was physical, in this passage "being made alive" and "being raised" are used metaphorically, referring to the spiritual existence possessed by believers that results from Christ's resurrection. The last verb, "being seated," is also used metaphorically to refer to "our present exaltation with the point of comparison being the privileges, honor, and authority involved with enthronement."[21] Lincoln rightly summarizes this parallel: "If raising Christ from death to sit in the heavenly realms was the supreme demonstration of God's surpassing power, then the raising of believers from spiritual death to sit with Christ in the heavenly realms is the supreme demonstration of God's surpassing grace."[22]

THE CAUSE OF REGENERATION

But what would compel God to take fallen, broken, and sinful humanity and give them the regenerating power of the Spirit? The answer in one word is *love*. Paul plainly tells us, "because of the great love with which he loved us . . ." (2:4). In fact, Paul emphasizes the origin of God's saving decision to rescue his people with a variety of phrases: "rich in mercy" (2:4), "great love" (2:4), "immeasurable riches of his grace" (2:7), and "kindness" (2:7). Salvation and new life are based solely on God's undeserved and unmerited favor. Thus our dire predicament changes because of God's mercy and his great love. God's merciful nature is clearly revealed in the Old Testament: "The LORD, the LORD, a God merciful and gracious, slow to anger, and abounding in steadfast love and faithfulness" (Ex. 34:6); "The LORD is merciful and gracious, slow to anger and abounding in steadfast love" (Ps. 103:8; see also Jonah 4:2). Elsewhere Paul states, "He saved us, not because of works done by us in righteousness, but according to his own mercy" (Titus 3:5). But God is not only merciful; he is also loving. Paul emphasizes God's love by supplying the adjective "great" and by reiterating his statement with the verbal form that follows ("with which he *loved* us"). Both God's mercy and his love are the causes that propelled him to awaken sinners by the regenerating work of the Spirit to bring new life to dead hearts.

Paul emphasizes that the cause of salvation (including regeneration) is *not* our good works. Salvation is "by grace" (Eph. 2:5, 8) and by grace alone. Grace is highlighted throughout Ephesians. Paul opens his letter

---

21   William J. Larkin, *Ephesians: A Handbook on the Greek Text*, BHGNT (Waco, TX: Baylor University Press, 2009), 32.

22   Lincoln, *Ephesians*, 110.

with a greeting of grace (1:2). God is to be praised because he has freely graced his people with glorious grace (1:6). We have redemption and forgiveness through the riches of his grace (1:7). Paul was a steward of God's grace (3:2, 8), a ministry itself that was received by grace (3:7, 8). Grace, and the resulting gift, is given to every believer through Christ (4:7). Instead of words to tear down, believers are exhorted to speak words that build up so "that it may give grace to those who hear" (4:29). Paul then ends his letter the way he began it, with a message of grace: "Grace be with all who love our Lord Jesus Christ with love incorruptible" (6:24).

Furthermore, this grace that results in regeneration is received *by* faith. There is an important distinction to make here. We are saved *because of* grace, which is attained *by means of* or *through* faith. That is, we are not saved because of or on the basis of faith. Faith does not save; God's grace based on Christ's atonement saves. Faith, then, is merely the instrument by which grace is received. As such, faith is not viewed as a meritorious work but trusts in Christ's life, death, and resurrection. Paul states negatively that salvation is "not your own doing" as well as "not a result of works" but positively it is "the gift of God" (2:8–9). If it is a gift, it is not earned but is freely received. Furthermore, if it is freely received as a gift and not dependent on good works, it precludes any boasting before God (see Rom. 3:27; Gal. 6:14; Phil. 3:3).

THE RESULT OF REGENERATION

As stated above, when God regenerates people, they are spiritually awakened, raised with Christ, and seated with him. God's regenerating work on an individual evokes a change of heart and a change of destiny. The divine purpose of God's act of granting new life and status to believers is so that "he might show the immeasurable riches of his grace" (Eph. 2:7). In 1:3–14 Paul stresses that the goal of bestowing every spiritual blessing upon believers is the glory of God (1:6, 12, 14). Here, Paul adds that God saves rebellious sinners in order to display or show off his grace, a grace that is highlighted with the adjective "immeasurable" and the noun "riches." But Paul mentions not only God's "mercy" (2:4), "love" (2:4), and "grace" (2:5, 7); he also includes God's "kindness" (2:7). Elsewhere, he explains that it is God's "kindness" that leads to repentance (Rom. 2:4) and that God chose to save us "when the goodness and loving kindness of God our Savior appeared" (Titus 3:4). God regenerates the dead hearts of sinners to publicly display his grace.

When people receive God's grace, they are spiritually awakened and indwelt by the Holy Spirit. Furthermore, God's quickening results in good works. As God's workmanship, believers were created to walk in good works as part of God's perfect plan (Eph. 2:10). The term "workmanship" (*poiēma*) designates God's work of the new creation (see 4:24; 2 Cor. 5:17; Gal. 6:15). Believers are not created anew based on their good works, but they are created anew for the purpose of good works, works that God predestined believers to perform (see Rom. 9:23). For Paul, the free and gracious nature of salvation leads to good works, not complacency or passivity. God's plan of salvation begins with grace and ends with grace.

God's Plan for the Apostle Paul

God's plan to unite all things in Christ and his plan to accomplish salvation among his people are both related to his plan in calling and using the apostle Paul. In other words, Paul becomes an essential component in revealing and executing God's plan for humanity. As the apostle to the Gentiles, Paul was given the task of revealing the mystery of God that was hidden in the past but made known through the life and ministry of Paul.

God's Calling of the Apostle Paul

APOSTLE

Paul begins Ephesians by identifying himself as an "apostle" (1:1), a technical use that is limited to the twelve (Matt. 10:2; Acts 1:2, 13; 1 Cor. 15:5, 7) and Paul (1 Cor. 9:1; 15:9). These apostles were chosen and commissioned by Jesus and therefore occupied a unique position as founders of the church. Paul specifies that he is an apostle "of Christ Jesus," a designation that indicates that Paul is one who belongs to and serves Jesus Christ. Thus he is fully authorized as Christ's messenger to proclaim the good news of the one who sent him. Additionally, his apostleship is "by the will of God." God is the one who chose and commissioned Paul to serve as an apostle to help build the church. At the time of his transformation and conversion, Paul was fighting against the church, seeking to destroy it (Gal. 1:13). The Lord conveyed to Ananias that Paul was indeed his "chosen instrument" who would carry his name before Gentiles, kings, and the children of Israel (Acts 9:15). Luke also records that the Lord told Paul that he appeared to Paul "to appoint" him as "a servant and witness" to bear testimony of God's grace to the Gentiles (Acts 26:16–18). As the apostle to the Gentiles, Paul was compelled to bring the gospel to major cities outside of Israel, including Ephesus. About five years after leaving Ephesus during his third missionary journey, Paul writes to "the saints" in Ephesus to assure them that the fruit of his labor has not been in vain. Paul's calling to reach the Gentiles with the gospel is not something that he gave himself, but something to which he was called according to the sovereign plan of God.[23]

PRISONER

Besides the designation of apostle, in chapter 3 Paul identifies his ministry using three other labels: prisoner, minister, and saint. Paul calls himself "a prisoner of Christ Jesus on behalf of you Gentiles" (3:1). Paul's reference to "prisoner" is literal, as Ephesians was written from prison, most likely in Rome where he was under arrest for two years (Acts 28:30). Elsewhere in this epistle, he identifies himself as "a prisoner for the Lord" (Eph. 4:1) and "an ambassador in chains" (6:20). Notably, Paul acknowledges that he is a prisoner of Jesus Christ and not Caesar since he belongs to Christ and is in prison for the sake of

---

23 It should be noted that some manuscripts do not include "in Ephesus." The ESV footnote reads, "Some manuscripts *saints who are also faithful* (omitting *in Ephesus*)." Consequently, some take "in Ephesus" to be a later (though still accurate) addition since the city of Ephesus was probably the first or primary location to which Paul's circular letter was sent. Others are convinced that the phrase is original.

the gospel. He further states that he is a prisoner "on behalf of you Gentiles" (3:1). Paul's imprisonment was not punishment for personal sin but due to his faithfulness in fulfilling his apostolic role of taking the gospel of Christ to the Gentiles.

MINISTER

Paul states that he "was made a minister" (*diakonos*) or servant of the gospel (3:7–8).[24] Paul provides a sevenfold emphasis that demonstrates that his role as God's servant was via divine appointment and not his own choice: (1) he uses a divine passive ("I was made"), which "underscores the idea that God put him into that service";[25] (2) his calling is called a "gift" (*dōrean*) or (3) "grace" (*charitos*); (4) he reiterates that the gift "was given," another divine passive; (5) God is designated as the source of the gift ("of God"); and (6) he elaborates that the grace he received is "by the working" of (7) God's "power." Elsewhere Paul confesses that although he "worked harder" than his contemporaries, he readily acknowledges that it was "by the grace of God" and that ultimately it was not him "but the grace of God" with him (1 Cor. 15:10). Paul viewed himself as a servant of the King who was given the commission to herald the good news of a Jewish Messiah who has provided a way of reconciliation with God.

SAINT

Finally, Paul designates himself as "the very least of all the saints" (Eph. 3:8). The term translated "very least" literally means "less than the least" or "the lessermost" and is a word that may have been coined by Paul himself.[26] So although he labels himself a "saint" (*hagios*), he views himself as the lowest of all the saints. In 1 Corinthians 15:9 he confesses that he is "the least of the apostles," and in 1 Timothy 1:15 he

---

24 See also 1 Cor. 3:5; 2 Cor. 3:6; 6:4; 11:23.

25 Harold W. Hoehner, *Ephesians: An Exegetical Commentary* (Grand Rapids, MI: Baker, 2002), 449.

26 Technically, this form is labeled a "comparative of the superlative." Daniel B. Wallace, *Greek Grammar Beyond the Basics* (Grand Rapids, MI: Zondervan, 1996), 302.

states that he is the "foremost" of all sinners. Paul recognizes that the commission to be Christ's ambassador to the nations was freely given to him by the grace of God and that he was an unworthy vessel as one who had persecuted the church (1 Cor. 15:9; 1 Tim. 1:13). Paul reiterates that the grace and calling he received were given to him by God (see Eph. 3:2, 7), which is what empowered him to fulfill his ministry to bring the good news of Christ to the Gentiles.

God's Revealing of the Mystery to Paul

THE CONTENT OF THE MYSTERY

What precisely is the mystery that was revealed to Paul? God chose to reveal a divine plan through Paul—an apostle, prisoner, minister, and the very least of all the saints. He refers to this privilege as a "stewardship" (*oikonomia*), which refers to his divine commission to preach the gospel to the nations (3:2). He further describes this stewardship as a grace from God (3:3, 7, 8). Three times in chapter 3 Paul refers to the "mystery" (3:3, 4, 9).[27] In 1:9–10 Paul stated that God made "known to us the mystery of his will," which included his plan "to unite all things" in Christ. In 3:6 he indicates the content of the mystery: "that the Gentiles are fellow heirs, members of the same body, and partakers of the promise."

Paul employs three compound terms to demonstrate that Gentiles are now on equal status with Jews: Gentiles are "fellow heirs" (*sygklēronoma*), "fellow body members" (*syssōma*), and "fellow partakers" (*symmetoxa*) in the promise.[28] "Fellow heirs" harkens back to the theme of adoption and inheritance in chapter 1 (1:5, 11, 14, 18; also see 5:5) and elsewhere in Paul's writings (Rom. 8:17; Gal. 3:18; Col. 3:24). It also recalls God's promise to bless all the families of the earth through Abraham (Gen. 12:3). "Fellow body members" ("members of the same body," ESV), implies that Gentile believers have been incorporated into

---

27 Some English translations such as the ESV and NIV add the word *mystery* to 3:6 in order to make clear that Paul is clarifying the nature of the mystery in that verse.

28 These are the author's translations of the terms in order to demonstrate the similarity of meaning.

the same body and have become "one new man" (Eph. 2:15) or "one body" (2:16). Now, both Jews and Gentiles together form the body of Christ, the church. Finally, "fellow partakers" ("partakers," ESV) "of the promise in Christ Jesus through the gospel" recalls the earlier reference that Gentiles were "strangers to the covenants of promise" (2:12). The promise could refer to either the Holy Spirit (see 1:13) or the blessings mentioned in God's promise to Abraham that would now also come to the Gentiles (see Gal. 3:8; Rom. 4:13). Perhaps both are in view since the gift of the Spirit and Abrahamic blessings are often merged together.[29] Paul adds that these blessings given to the Gentiles are attainable only by being united to Christ through faith. In Ephesians 3:4 Paul refers to the mystery as the "mystery of Christ," which probably indicates that it is a mystery that involves Christ. Thus the mystery is specifically related to the Jews and Gentiles being united with the body of Christ to form the one people of God. Although the Old Testament reveals God's plan to bless the nations through his covenant with Abraham, we now know that the nations (Gentiles) are blessed as part of the one people of God, united with Jews on an equal basis to form one body.

THE TIMING OF THE MYSTERY

From the beginning, God had a plan to bless Abraham and, through him, the nations. Certain elements of this plan, however, were not disclosed, especially how Gentiles would become one body with Jews. But at the perfect time, God unveiled his plan. Paul declares that he received this insight "by revelation" (3:3; see Gal. 1:12), which probably refers to his Damascus road experience. Paul was not only commissioned to preach the gospel to the nations (Eph. 3:8), but he was also called to reveal God's mystery (3:9). As Paul preached the unsearchable riches of Christ in the gospel to the Gentiles, those who repented and believed were reconciled to God through his Son and became fellow members of the body of Christ with Jewish believers.

29 See Eph. 1:13; Isa. 32:15; 44:3; Ezek. 11:19; 36:26–27; 37:14; Joel 3:1–2.

In 3:5 Paul clarifies that the mystery is something that was previously unknown: "[The mystery] was not made known to the sons of men in other generations as it has now been revealed to his holy apostles and prophets by the Spirit." Note the timing of the mystery: it was not revealed to previous generations but has now been revealed by the Spirit of God to his people through the apostles and prophets. Paul is not implying that the Old Testament lacks any reference to blessings that would come to the Gentiles (see Gen. 12:3; 22:18; 26:4; 28:14) or to the future inclusion of the Gentiles within Israel (see Lev. 19:34; Deut. 10:18–19; 1 Kings 8:41–43). Rather, the meaning is that no prophet ever announced that these two groups would be joined together as one people and form the body of Christ. In Ephesians 3:9 Paul explains that his calling was "to bring to light for everyone what is the plan of the mystery hidden for ages in God." By "hidden," Paul is referring to that which was planned by God but not yet revealed to his people. That is, it was hidden from past ages but only resided in the mind of God. As the sovereign Creator, God would ensure that his once-hidden plan was carried out according to his perfect design. What was hidden is "now" (3:10) made known, suggesting a new salvation-historical era has begun. Specifically, this plan was "realized in Christ Jesus our Lord" (3:11). God's plan of redemption, though not fully complete, has been revealed and centers on Christ, who will "unite all things" (1:10).

God's Plan in Prayer

Prayer is also an important part of God's plan for his people. Twice in Ephesians Paul prays for his readers (1:15–23; 3:14–21), and once he exhorts them to pray, including praying for Paul himself (6:18–20; see also 5:20). In this letter, he refers to God as Father eight times,[30] once in each of his prayers ("Father of glory," 1:17; "the Father," 3:14) and once when he exhorts his readers to be filled with the Spirit, "giving thanks always and for everything to God the Father in the name of our Lord Jesus Christ" (5:20). As a gracious Father, God loves to hear the

---

30 References to God as Father: 1:2, 3, 17; 2:18; 3:14; 4:6; 5:20; 6:23.

prayers of his children. Believers offer prayers to God, not so much to change God's mind (though certainly "the prayer of a righteous person has great power as it is working," James 5:16) but to ask God to change us and give us the mind of Christ. Interestingly, Paul does not focus his prayers on what believers should do but on how they should think. This is not because doing is unimportant but because correct thinking leads to obedience. Thus Paul often prays that God would open the eyes and hearts of his readers so that they may be enlightened, know, comprehend, and think in line with God's promises and God's plans.

Paul's First Prayer

After an extended blessing of God (Eph. 1:3–14), Paul offers a prayer of thanksgiving for the faith and love of his readers (1:15–19). Before giving the content of the prayer, he provides a twofold description of the one who is the source of all blessings: he is "the God of our Lord Jesus Christ" and "the Father of glory" (1:17). Specifically, Paul prays that God would give his people "the Spirit of wisdom and of revelation" (1:17). Although some take "spirit" as a reference to the human disposition,[31] it is best to understand it as a designation of the Holy Spirit who imparts wisdom and revelation to God's people (see Isa. 11:2). Arnold notes, "What Paul is referring to here is not new truths about salvation history, the nature of God, or other doctrine, but an illuminating work of the Spirit to impress already revealed truth about God into the conscious reflections and heartfelt convictions of the readers."[32] So Paul prays that the Spirit will produce both wisdom and knowledge so that they will comprehend the unfolding plan of God.

In Ephesians 1:18–19 Paul further unpacks the work of the Spirit. Namely, that he would grant his readers spiritual insight, "having the eyes of [their] hearts enlightened" (1:18). This phrase most likely refers to the ability to discern spiritual realities related to the purpose and plan of God (see Pss. 13:3; 19:8). Paul then prays specifically that his readers

---

31 See CSB, NASB, NRSV; cf. Rom. 8:15; 11:8; 1 Cor. 4:21; Gal. 6:1; Eph. 4:23; 2 Tim. 1:7.
32 Arnold, *Ephesians*, 105.

will comprehend three spiritual realities. First, he prays that they will know the hope to which God has called them. God has elected his people (Eph. 1:4), called them through the word of Christ (Rom. 8:30; 10:17), and now offers hope in that gospel (Col. 1:5). Previously they were estranged from God's people and had "no hope" (Eph. 2:12). Through Christ's atoning and redemptive work on the cross, the hopeless have become hopeful, and so Paul prays that in faith they will believe all that God has promised to them. Second, Paul prays that they will know the riches of their glorious inheritance (see earlier section "Inheritance (Adoption)"). Third, he wants them to know the immeasurable greatness of God's power, especially as it is displayed in Christ. That is, the same power that raised Jesus from the dead, seated him at God's right hand in power, and gave him authority over the cosmos is the same power at work in believers (1:20–22). Paul stresses the power of God when he speaks of the "immeasurable greatness" of God's "power," which is in accordance with "the working" of his "great might" (1:19). These terms are piled up to provoke the readers' confidence in God and his plan for their lives.

Paul's Second Prayer

In 3:14–21 Paul offers a second prayer for his audience. Instead of using a verb for *praying*, he describes the action of bowing or bending his knees before the Father. Like his previous prayer, Paul concentrates on their thoughts and attitudes. He offers a prayer for (1) strength, (2) understanding, and (3) filling.

First, Paul prays that his readers would "be strengthened with power through his Spirit" in their inner being (3:16). This strength is "according to the riches of his glory," indicating a limitless resource (see also Phil. 4:19). Thus God is graciously and lavishly supplying all the strength that believers need. This strengthening is "with power" and through the agency of "his Spirit" (Eph. 3:16). The result of being strengthened is that the continual presence of Christ "may dwell" in their hearts (3:17).

Second, Paul prays for his readers to understand and experience the love of Christ. In order to attain this understanding, believers must be "rooted and grounded" in God's amazing love (3:17). Paul desires each Christian to grasp the immense love of Christ for them. His main petition is that believers "may have strength to comprehend" and "know the love of Christ" (3:18–19). The dimensions of breadth, length, height, and depth all function to describe the immensity of God's love for his people (see Rom. 8:35–39). Paul qualifies Christ's love for believers as a love that "surpasses knowledge" (Eph. 3:19). Paradoxically, Paul prays that the Ephesian Christians would be able to know and comprehend something that is incomprehensible. Thus the love of Christ is so vast that it can never be exhausted or fully grasped.

Finally, Paul requests that they "be filled with all the fullness of God" (3:19). That is, believers should long to be filled up to and with the very fullness of God. Similarly, in 4:13 Paul states that believers are to attain "to the measure of the stature of the fullness of Christ" (see also 1:23; Col. 1:19; 2:9). It is likely that the "fullness" of God refers to God's moral excellence or perfections, including his love. Later, Paul will exhort his readers to "walk in love" (Eph. 5:2).

Paul ends this prayer with a doxology (3:20–21). Although Paul focuses his prayers on the need for Christians to be mentally grounded in the reality of God's gracious plan and God's unending love, his doxology demonstrates that we will never fully comprehend or understand this reality since God "is able to do far more abundantly than all that we ask or think" (3:20). God is able not only to do what we imagine (or even more than we imagine) but "far more abundantly" than we could even imagine. This rare adjective (*hyperekperissou*) means "quite beyond all measure" and communicates "the highest form of comparison imaginable."[33] This same God is "at work within us" (3:20). Consequently, our response should be to praise and glorify God.

Paul's Exhortation to Pray and Request for Prayer

As Paul closes his letter, he exhorts his readers to take their stand, putting on the full armor of God. His final command is that they pray,

33 BDAG 1033.

including praying for Paul himself. God's plan for believers is that they trust in the strength that he provides, which is not possible without fervent prayer. Believers "stand" by kneeling in prayer. In fact, it seems that Paul is suggesting that the way in which believers arm themselves against the enemy is through prayer. This call to prayer is emphasized several ways (6:18). First, believers should pray "at all times." Even as Paul himself has prayed for his readers twice in this letter, so too Christians should make it a practice of constantly praying throughout the day (see 1 Thess. 5:17). Second, they should pray "in the Spirit" since it is the Holy Spirit who leads and strengthens believers to pray. Arnold writes, "The Spirit stands by the side of believers to prompt them to pray, to direct them whom to pray for and how to pray, as well as to energize them in praying for themselves and others."[34] Third, believers should pray "with all prayer and supplication." The repetition of prayer terminology emphasizes the importance of praying diligently and expectantly. Fourth, they are to "keep alert." They must stay vigilant even in the midst of intense warfare. Fifth, they are to be alert and pray "with all perseverance," refusing to give up when there are no tangible results. Finally, they are to pray "for all the saints." Believers must pray for each other to stand firm against the attacks of the enemy.

Paul not only encourages believers to pray for each other; he also solicits prayer for himself (Eph. 6:19), which is not unusual for Paul (see Rom. 15:30–32; 2 Cor. 1:11; Col. 4:3–4; 1 Thess. 5:25; 2 Thess. 3:1–2). Astonishingly, he does not request that he be released from his imprisonment but instead asks that he would be faithful and bold to share the gospel freely and clearly with others: "that words may be given to me in opening my mouth boldly to proclaim the mystery of the gospel" (Eph. 6:19). Paul thus asks for prayer to courageously do the very thing that led to his arrest and him being "an ambassador in chains" (6:20; see also 2 Cor. 5:20). Paul views himself as an official representative of God with the specific calling and commission to preach the mystery of the gospel to the Gentiles (see Eph. 3:2, 7–8).

34 Arnold, *Ephesians*, 464.

And so Paul requests that he will be faithful to his calling and the gospel to "declare it boldly." Paul later indicates the Lord stood by him and strengthened him so that he was able to proclaim the message faithfully to the Gentiles (2 Tim. 4:17).

In prayer believers are asking God to help them trust and rely on his strength. In prayer believers are trusting in God's purpose and plan to obediently follow God's revealed truth. In prayer believers are praying for others to be faithful to what God has called them to do. In prayer believers should be seeking to follow God's will and not their own will.

Summary

God is the creator and sustainer of the universe. He is the Alpha and the Omega, the beginning and the end (Rev. 1:8; 21:6; 22:13). Nothing is hidden from him "but all are naked and exposed" before him (Heb. 4:13). With patience and great wisdom, he works "all things according to the counsel of his will" (Eph. 1:11). His plan ultimately includes uniting all things in Christ since the Son is the center and focus of the divine plan. God's plan in salvation to elect, regenerate, redeem, adopt, and seal believers is based on his great love and the finished work of Christ. His plan included calling the apostle Paul and revealing to him the divine mystery that included the uniting of both Jew and Gentile into the one people of God. Finally, his plan includes a praying people as was demonstrated by Paul's two prayers in this letter as well as his exhortation for believers to pray and his own personal request for prayer.

2

Union with Christ

ALTHOUGH IT MAY NOT BE POSSIBLE TO identify one particular topic as *the* central theme in Paul's theology, it is possible to locate central or key themes that occupy critical importance.

Union with Christ in Paul

In his work *Paul and Union with Christ: An Exegetical and Theological Study*, Constantine Campbell uses the helpful analogy of a web in regard to the place of union with Christ in Paul's thought. Unlike a wheel that has spokes emanating from a clearly defined center, a web has a series of concentric circles. Thus he argues that union with Christ is not the center of Paul's theology, but it is a key teaching that provides the "webbing" that holds it all together. As such, it provides a crucial element that has been neglected or misunderstood. Though it may not be the center of Paul's thought, it is intricately connected to everything else.[1] It is the glue that holds various aspects of salvation together. Campbell concludes, "Every Pauline theme and pastoral concern coheres with the whole through their common bond—union with Christ."[2]

---

1 Dunn maintains that in contrast to justification, participation in Christ "is in many ways the more natural extension of Paul's Christology" since it is much more pervasive (James D. G. Dunn, *The Theology of Paul the Apostle* [Grand Rapids, MI: Eerdmans, 1998], 390). He later adds that "the study of participation in Christ leads more directly into the rest of Paul's theology than justification" (395).

2 Constantine R. Campbell, *Paul and Union with Christ: An Exegetical and Theological Study* (Grand Rapids, MI: Zondervan, 2012), 441.

Paul references union with Christ approximately two hundred times, with about forty of those found in Ephesians.[3] The most common uses include "in Christ" (*en Christō*) and "in the Lord" (*en Kyriō*),[4] but other less common uses are "with Christ" (*syn Christō*),[5] "into Christ" (*eis Christō*), and metaphors such as the body and temple of Christ. The phrase "in Jesus" occurs once (in Eph. 4:21), and although "in Christ Jesus" is found, the phrase "in Jesus Christ" never occurs. Seifrid offers the following nuances regarding the significance of various expressions:

> The prominence of "Christ" in the phrase suggests an emphasis on the exalted status and saving role of the Messiah. The frequently attached name "Jesus" may call forth the idea of the earthly figure and his humanity. The alternative form "in the Lord" usually stresses the unique power and divine authority of Christ, and hence his right to demand obedience or his ability to deliver from other "powers."[6]

Seifrid summarizes Paul's varied usage of union with Christ:

- More than a third of the references relate to salvation.
- Approximately another third relate to exhortations of behavior or character.
- About twenty designate the present state of believers in view of Christ's saving work.
- About twelve describe specific persons or particular situations in relation to salvation.
- Two are related strictly to the nature of Christ (Col. 1:19; 2:9).[7]

3   A. M. Hunter, *The Gospel according to Paul* (Philadelphia: Westminster Press, 1954), 37 ("some 200 times"); Seifrid claims 151 references (Mark A. Seifrid, "In Christ," in *DPL* 436). These occurrences are found in all of Paul's letters except Titus (see Leon Morris, *New Testament Theology* [Grand Rapids, MI: Zondervan, 1986], 51).

4   According to Dunn, "in Christ" occurs eighty-three times in Paul's letters (thirteen in Ephesians), not counting pronouns such as "in him" or "in whom," and "in the Lord" forty-seven times (eight in Ephesians). *Theology of Paul the Apostle*, 396–97.

5   This also includes verbs that have "with" compounds such as found in Eph. 2:5, 6.

6   Seifrid, "In Christ," 433.

7   Seifrid, "In Christ," 436.

Union with Christ is a prominent or key theme in Paul's writings, especially in Ephesians (and Colossians). This theme will be explored in more detail in the following sections.

The Meaning of Union with Christ

But what precisely is meant by "union with Christ"? Historically, some have preferred the terms *mysticism, union,* or *participation.* In Paul's writings, however, one term is not able to fully capture the breadth of nuances in the various uses. Based on his extensive inductive study, Campbell settles on these four concepts: union, participation, identification, and incorporation. He explains: "*Union* gathers up faith union with Christ, mutual indwelling, trinitarian, and nuptial notions. *Participation* conveys partaking in the events of Christ's narrative. *Identification* refers to believers' location in the realm of Christ and their allegiance to his lordship. *Incorporation* encapsulates the corporate dimensions of membership in Christ's body."[8] Using the categories set out by Campbell, the following section will detail specific occurrences, highlighting their theological significance.

Union

First, union with Christ can refer to believers being united to Christ by faith through the work of the Spirit. Historically, this has been called "the mystical union with Christ." It is not a physical or ontological union but is a spiritual union through the indwelling and activity of the Holy Spirit. And yet this union is not merely supposed or theoretical but is an actual union. Although most of the time the believer is said to be "in Christ," occasionally Christ is said to indwell believers (Gal. 2:20; Col. 1:27), illustrating a concept of mutual indwelling. Paul occasionally uses the analogy of marriage and the nuptial union to communicate mutual indwelling. In this section, several key texts will be discussed, including Ephesians 1:9–10; 6:10, as well as the marriage analogy in 5:22–32.

---

8   Campbell, *Paul and Union with Christ,* 413; emphasis original.

Ephesians 1 has the highest concentration of "in Christ" language in the letter, especially 1:3–14, which has eleven occurrences. In the previous chapter we discussed the central statement and high point of the opening eulogy regarding God's plan to unite all things *in Christ*. It should be noted that this "in Christ" language does not involve a believer's union with Christ but Christ's union with the Father. In 1:9–10 Paul specifies that God has made known "the mystery of his will, according to his purpose, which he set forth in Christ [*en autō*, literally "in him"] as a plan for the fullness of time, to unite all things in him, things in heaven and things on earth." God's decision and purpose were set forth and planned *in Christ*. Put differently, Christ was intimately involved in planning the redemption with the Father. The Father and the Son have a close connection and shared purpose. When the Father made and revealed his plans for the cosmos, it was done in conjunction and union with the Son. Union with Christ was not something newly established for the church, but it existed before time began. The Father's purpose was not done in isolation but was achieved through the unity of the Godhead.

Another text that highlights the union with Christ is the marriage metaphor found in 5:22–32. Unlike the previous passage (1:9–10), this passage focuses on the believer's union with Christ (instead of the Father's union with the Son). As Paul encourages wives to submit to their husbands and husbands to love their wives, he compares the marriage relationship to the relationship between Christ and his bride, the church. Thus in this analogy Christ is depicted as a faithful husband of the church.

> For the husband is the head of the wife even as Christ is the head of the church, his body, and is himself its Savior. (5:23)

> For no one ever hated his own flesh, but nourishes and cherishes it, just as Christ does the church, because we are members of his body. (5:29–30)

Specifically, in these verses the church is designated as the *body*.[9] Christ is the head of the body (the church) just as a husband is head of his wife. Not only is Christ the head of the church, but he is also "its Savior" (5:23) because he redeemed her for himself. Those who are united to Christ through faith are spiritually joined to him and become his bride. Believers are to submit to Christ because he is their head and their Savior. He is the one who loves his bride, who laid down his life to redeem her ("gave himself up for her," 5:25), and will one day present her holy and blameless (5:27). He is the one who "nourishes and cherishes" her as his own (5:29). Hoehner writes, "He redeemed it (1:7–12; 2:1–10), sealed it (1:13–14), empowered it (1:19–23), brought it into one body (2:16), filled it with God's fullness (3:19), gifted it (4:7–16), and loved and sanctified it (5:25–26). . . . Christ . . . is not only a ruler or authority over the church but also the source of sustenance by which it is nurtured."[10] He does this because as the church, his bride, "we are members of his body" (5:30). By their union with Christ, believers are part of the body of Christ.

Paul metaphorically depicts the relationship between Christ and his church as a marriage. He is united to her as a husband and wife are united and thus become "one flesh" (5:31, quoting Gen. 2:24). In case there was any doubt about the reality of Paul's analogy, he clarifies, "This mystery is profound, and I am saying that it refers to Christ and the church" (5:32). The Christ-church relationship is termed a "mystery," which refers to the once-hidden plan of God that is now revealed in Jesus.[11] Further, Paul labels this mystery "profound" or great (*megas*), thereby emphasizing the significance or magnitude of the mystery. Just as the first Adam was joined to his wife and became one flesh with her, so too the last Adam is joined with his bride so that he becomes one flesh with her. The one-flesh spiritual union for Christ and the church becomes the model of the one-flesh physical union of a husband and

9 See also Eph. 1:23; 2:16; 4:4, 12, 16.
10 Harold W. Hoehner, *Ephesians: An Exegetical Commentary* (Grand Rapids, MI: Baker, 2002), 768.
11 See also Eph. 1:9; 3:3–4, 9; 6:19.

wife. Note that Paul argues from Christ's relationship with the church as a pattern for human marital relationships and not vice versa.

Several implications can be drawn out from this passage regarding a believer's spiritual union with Christ.[12] First, just as the intimate bond between a husband and wife does not eliminate personal distinctions, neither does the union between Christ and the church. Paul's analogy does not suggest some sort of vague mysticism where a believer is absorbed into the divine, but within this spiritual union each partner maintains a distinct role. Second, the church is called to submit to Christ, her head. This one-flesh union still maintains Christ's headship as Lord and also calls the church to humble obedience. Third, Christ is the one who completely provides for his bride. He saves her (5:23), loves her (5:25), gave himself for her (5:25), makes her holy (5:26), presents her as blameless (5:27), and nourishes and cherishes her (5:29). Campbell summarizes: "All of this underscores the reality that the one-flesh union with Christ is instigated by grace; it is not a union that believers 'achieve' or approach through mystical disciplines or spiritual advancement."[13] The church's relationship with Christ is based on grace and grace alone.

A third text that speaks of a believer's union with Christ is 6:10: "Finally, be strong in the Lord and in the strength of his might." As Paul concludes his letter, he urges his readers to find their strength in the Lord. Thus he both commands them to action ("be strong") but also reminds them that their power comes from an external source ("in the Lord"; see also 3:16). When Paul says to be strong *in the Lord* he is referring to believers' union with Christ, which is their only source of power. Paul emphasizes Christ's power over satanic forces by adding "and in the strength of his might." Because the armor that Paul lists not only suggests images of Roman weaponry but also echoes the description of the armor that Yahweh wears in battle,[14] one of the implications

---

12 The following implications are summarized from Campbell, *Paul and Union with Christ*, 308–9.

13 Campbell, *Paul and Union with Christ*, 309.

14 See, e.g., Isa. 11:4–5 (LXX).

"is that believers are to put on the armour that the Lord himself wears in battle, which evokes a sense of union with him in the matter of spiritual warfare."[15] In the midst of intense spiritual warfare, the strength to battle and stand firm against the schemes of the enemy is based on the believer's spiritual union with the resurrected and ascended Christ.

Participation

Second, union with Christ can emphasize believers' participation in the redemptive events of Christ's narrative, namely his death, burial, resurrection, ascension, and glorification. In English, these texts will typically be translated as "with" Christ instead of "in" Christ. Because of their spiritual union *in* Christ through faith, they are also counted as being *with* Christ as he defeated death, rose from the dead, ascended to heaven, and was glorified as the conquering Son. It is as if believers partook of and accomplished all that Christ accomplished.

The key text in Ephesians that conveys the idea of participation with Christ is found in 2:5–6:

> [But God . . . ,] even when we were dead in our trespasses, made us alive together *with Christ*—by grace you have been saved—and raised us up with him and seated us *with him* in the heavenly places *in Christ Jesus.*

Paul identifies three ways in which believers participate in Christ's acts of redemption, all communicated by the use of three compound verbs that contain the same prepositional prefix *syn-*: *synezōopoiēsen, synēgeiren,* and *synekathisen.* The preposition *syn* communicates the meaning of "together with." That which God accomplishes for believers was first accomplished in Christ. Paul states first that those who are united to Christ by faith are "made alive together with" Christ. This verb (*synezōopoiēsen*) occurs in only one other passage in the New Testament. In Colossians 2:13 Paul similarly writes, "And you, who

---

15 Campbell, *Paul and Union with Christ*, 153.

were dead in your trespasses and the uncircumcision of your flesh, God made alive together [*synezōopoiēsen*] with him, having forgiven us all our trespasses." The spiritual state of all people without the life-awakening power of God is one of deadness. Earlier he reminds his readers that they "were dead in [their] trespasses and sins" (Eph. 2:1). Before conversion, all humanity (including believers) lived in rebellion against God, being dead to the things of God and powerless to truly obey from the heart. Paul clarifies that believers are made alive "with Christ."[16] Here the focus is not so much the mystical union with Christ but the believer participating in an event that Christ himself experienced. Believers receive new life because they participate in what happened to Christ. Lincoln notes, "A relationship with Christ is in view which affects believers' future destinies because it involves sharing in Christ's destiny."[17]

Although not specifically referenced in this passage, Paul elsewhere explains that sharing in Christ's life also means sharing in his death. For example, in Romans 6 Paul reminds his readers that their faith unites them to Christ's death, which includes death to the old order of sin and its dominion or power over them. Using baptism language Paul states:

We were buried therefore with him by baptism into death, in order that, just as Christ was raised from the dead by the glory of the Father, we too might walk in newness of life. For if we have been united with him in a death like his, we shall certainly be united with him in a resurrection like his. We know that our old self was crucified with him in order that the body of sin might be brought to nothing, so that we would no longer be enslaved to sin. For one who has died has been set free from sin. Now if we have died with Christ, we believe that we will also live with him. (Rom. 6:4–8)

16 The Greek phrase *tō Christō* is a dative of association, which is common when used in construction with compound verbs with a *syn* ("together with") prefix. See Daniel B. Wallace, *Greek Grammar beyond the Basics* (Grand Rapids, MI: Zondervan, 1996), 160.

17 Andrew D. Lincoln, *Ephesians*, WBC 42 (Dallas: Word, 1990), 101.

So in Paul's thought, we not only are made alive with Christ, but we are also united with him in his death, which results in sin not having power to dominate a believer.[18] Paul also emphasizes the present suffering of those united with Christ. Believers are "heirs of God and fellow heirs [sygklēronomoi] with Christ, provided we suffer with him [sympaschomen] in order that we may also be glorified with him [syndoksasthōmen]" (Rom. 8:17; see also Phil. 3:10).[19]

Paul continues by declaring that Christians are not only made alive but also are "raised . . . up with" (synēgeiren) and "seated . . . with" (synekathisen) Christ (Eph. 2:6). These two verbs recall Paul's earlier statement in the previous chapter that God "raised" Christ from the dead and "seated" him in heaven at his right hand (1:20). Just as Christ was physically raised from the dead, believers are spiritually raised. This verb is thus metaphorical of the resurrection life that is proleptically experienced by those united with Christ. They participate in his experience. "What God did for Christ he did at the same time for believers."[20] Because Christ is the representative head of a new humanity, what God accomplished for him, he also accomplished for those who are united to him.

Furthermore, those united to Christ are seated with Christ in the heavens. In Colossians Paul states that believers should seek those things that are above since that is where Christ is (Col. 3:1). Believers are raised and seated with Christ (Eph. 2:6), taking part in the benefits of Christ's resurrection and exaltation. Noticeably missing is the phrase "at his right hand" (1:20; cf. Col. 3:1) since that place is reserved only for the unique Son of God. Thus what Paul is referring to in Ephesians 2:5–6 is not a subjective experience of believers but their partnership in the events of redemptive history. Because believers have died with Christ, have been made alive and raised with him, and have been seated in heaven with him, "they are part of the new dominion's superiority over the old, participating in its liberation from the powers and its

---

18 See also Gal. 2:19–20; Col. 2:12, 20; 3:1.
19 Each one of the verbs contains the *syn* ("together with") prefix.
20 Lincoln, *Ephesians*, 105.

restoration of harmony to the cosmos."[21] The future reign of Christ has already broken into the present, giving believers the power to overcome the power of sin, the flesh, and the devil in this present age because of their participation with Christ.

Identification

Third, union with Christ can denote the believer's identification with (or in the realm of) Christ. As such, believers are designated as being under the dominion and rule of Christ and are thus expected to live under his authority. No longer are believers "in Adam" with lives shaped by sin and death, but they are "in Christ," owing their allegiance solely to him. They are no longer slaves to sin but live under the lordship of a new master, Christ, the second Adam. Because they are in the realm of Christ (and thus identified with him), they are beneficiaries of God's lavish grace.

Paul references this nuance of union in Christ at least seven times in five verses within chapter 1:

> . . . to the praise of his glorious grace, with which he has blessed us *in the Beloved. In him* we have redemption through his blood, the forgiveness of our trespasses, according to the riches of his grace . . . as a plan for the fullness of time, to unite all things *in [Christ]*, things in heaven and things on earth *[in him]. In him* we have obtained an inheritance, having been predestined according to the purpose of him who works all things according to the counsel of his will. . . . *In him* you also, when you heard the word of truth, the gospel of your salvation, and believed *in him*, were sealed with the promised Holy Spirit. (1:6–7, 10–11, 13)[22]

Although 1:3–14 has already been treated in chapter 1 ("The Plan of God"), union with Christ is a dominant subtheme in this passage. In

---

21 Lincoln, *Ephesians*, 108–9.
22 Eph. 1:10 has two uses of "in Christ/him" in the Greek, which is not expressed in the ESV.

fact, union with Christ is usually not the main topic of discourse but often functions like a thread that is woven into the fabric of discussion. Or, to use other analogies, it is the foundation upon which other truths are built, or the headwaters from which the currents of life flow. In this passage Paul erupts with praise to God because God has shown his rich mercy to those who are in Christ: he chooses us (1:4–5), redeems and forgives us (1:7), adopts us and gives us an inheritance (1:5, 11), and seals us with the Holy Spirit (1:13). When people are united to Christ, their identity before God changes. They become part of God's family and receive all the blessings and privileges that belong to Christ.

In 1:6 Paul expresses that God's blessings to believers come because of their identification with "the Beloved." Because Jesus is the beloved Son, so too Christians are beloved of God and receive blessings from him. In Colossians 1:13 Paul similarly states that God "has delivered us from the domain of darkness and transferred us to the kingdom of his beloved Son." Believers are chosen, adopted, redeemed, and forgiven because of their union and identification with Christ. It should be noted that the usage of "in Christ/him" in Ephesians 1:10 is different from all the other uses since it envisions the renewal of *all things* in Christ, and not just believers. Here, Christ becomes the center and focus to which all things are drawn and unified. He is not merely the agent (*by whom*) or the instrument (*through whom*) that brings unity, but he himself is the location (*in whom*) all this occurs. Finally, in 1:11 and 13 Paul adds that union with Christ includes receiving a future inheritance and being sealed with the Spirit. When our identity is in Christ, we receive all that was promised to him because of his faithfulness and obedience.

The following three texts also emphasize identification in Christ:

But now *in Christ Jesus* you who once were far off have been brought near by the blood of Christ. (2:13)

This mystery is that the Gentiles are fellow heirs, members of the same body, and partakers of the promise *in Christ Jesus* through the gospel. (3:6)

> For at one time you were darkness, but now you are light *in the Lord*.
> Walk as children of light. (5:8)

Believers, specifically referring to Gentiles in these passages, have been brought near to God and his people (2:13), are partakers of the promise (3:6), and are now light (5:8). Paul calls Gentiles to remember their past so that they can delight in their present and future. They were once separated from Christ, excluded from citizenship with God's people, strangers to God's covenants, and thus had no hope because they were without God (2:12). But now, because they have been united and identified with Christ by his blood, they are no longer far from God but have been brought near and reconciled to him (2:13).

God chose to reveal the mystery of the gospel—that Jew and Gentile together form the one people of God through their common faith in Christ—to the apostle Paul (3:6). That is, the Gentiles are "fellow heirs," "members of the same body," and "partakers" of the same promise, a promise that is gained through union with Christ. Thus these blessings that come to Gentile Christians are linked with union and identification with Christ. It is only through faith in Christ that these blessings can be attained.

Finally, Paul references an amazing transformation in 5:8: those who were once darkness are now light. Darkness is the realm of sin and evil, and we know that "God is light, and in him is no darkness at all" (1 John 1:5). This transference from one domain to another is not based on the moral power of a person. Rather, union with Christ is what makes the difference. Because the parallel phrase regarding darkness is not qualified ("you were darkness"), the addition of the prepositional phrase ("you are light *in the Lord*") suggests that believers' union with Christ is what makes the difference in their new state. All those who are united to Christ by faith are identified with Christ. They live under his rule and wholeheartedly give their allegiance to him. Consequently, they receive the richest blessings both in this life and in the one to come.

Incorporation

Fourth, union with Christ can also designate the community of believers who are united together through their mutual commitment to and trust in Christ. Metaphors such as body, temple, church, and building are used to convey this concept. Because believers are grafted into a new community with Christ as their founder and leader, they must seek to live in such a way that honors both Christ and other members, since by being united to Christ they are also united to each other. Two major texts that communicate this aspect of union with Christ include Ephesians 2:14–22 and 4:1–16.

First, in the second half of chapter 2, Paul employs two metaphors to demonstrate the unity of Jews and Gentiles: the body and the temple or building. The first time Paul uses the body metaphor in connection with the church is in chapter 1 when he states, "And he put all things under his feet and gave him as head over all things to the church, which is his body, the fullness of him who fills all in all" (1:22–23). The church is Christ's body, and he is head over all things for the church. Although Christ and believers make up one body with Christ as head, in this metaphor there still remains a distinction between the two. Believers are thus united to Christ and share in his fullness while at the same time remain distinct from the head who is Christ. Just as believers are all part of one body and yet remain distinct, so too Christ as the head of the body maintains his own person. As such, believers who are united to Christ also remain under his authority.

Then in 2:16 Paul once again picks up the body metaphor, though applying it differently. He states that Christ has torn down the dividing wall of hostility (2:14) so that he "might reconcile us both to God in *one body* through the cross" (2:16). This phrase "one body" most likely refers to the church, which parallels the "one" of 2:14 and the "one new man" of 2:15.[23] In Colossians 3:15 Paul writes, "And let the peace of Christ rule in your hearts, to which indeed you were called in one body. And

23 It is possible that the "in one body" parallels "in his flesh" (2:14) and "in himself" (2:15) and thus refers to Christ's physical body and not the church. See Campbell, *Paul and Union with Christ*, 278–79.

be thankful." Here, the phrase "one body" clearly refers to the church, and so it is likely that it does in Ephesians as well. The specific language of union with Christ is found in 2:15 where Paul clarifies that Christ made both Jew and Gentile one, abolishing the law "that he might create *in himself* one new man." That is, Jew and Gentile are incorporated into Christ, becoming consolidated into one new entity. Gentiles who were formerly far away from God (i.e., without Christ, excluded from Israel, foreigners to the covenants, and without God) have now been brought near to God through Christ's atoning blood (2:12–13). Those who were excluded and separated are now unified and incorporated into God's people. Jew and Gentile are now reconciled and incorporated into the church, the body of Christ.

Later in this passage, Paul moves from the body to the temple and building metaphor. He writes:

> So then you are no longer strangers and aliens, but you are fellow citizens with the saints and members of the household of God, built on the foundation of the apostles and prophets, Christ Jesus himself being the cornerstone, *in whom* the whole structure, being joined together, grows into a holy temple *in the Lord. In him* you also are being built together into a dwelling place for God by the Spirit. (2:19–22)

Paul emphasizes the unity, reception, and incorporation of Gentiles into the people of God using several word pictures. They are "fellow citizens," "members of the household" of God (2:19), a "structure" that grows into a "holy temple" (2:21), and a "dwelling place" for God (2:22). By their faith in Christ, Gentile Christians are fully accepted by God as part of the one messianic community. Furthermore, three words containing *syn* ("together with") also add to the Jew-Gentile unity. Gentiles are called "fellow citizens" (*sympolitai*) who are "being joined together" (*synarmologoumenē*) and "are being built together" (*synoikodomeisthe*). Finally, three references to union with Christ also are found here: "in whom" (2:21), "in the Lord" (2:21), and "in him" (2:22). Campbell notes the Trinitarian emphasis in this text: "The temple is *in the Lord* and built for *God's dwelling in the Spirit.*"[24] Thus the work of the Trinity is involved in uniting and incorporating Jews and Gentiles into the one people of God.

Second, the body metaphor is also used several times in Ephesians 4:

There is *one body* and one Spirit—just as you were called to the one hope that belongs to your call. (4:4)

And he gave the apostles, the prophets, the evangelists, the shepherds and teachers, to equip the saints for the work of ministry, for building up the *body of Christ.* (4:11–12)

Rather, speaking the truth in love, we are to grow up in every way into him who is the head, into Christ, from whom the *whole body,* joined and held together by every joint with which it is equipped, when each part is working properly, makes the *body* grow so that it builds itself up in love. (4:15–16)

In these texts, the references to *the body* all refer to the church. In the context of 4:4, Paul is discussing the unity of believers, and so he stresses the oneness of the Christian faith: there is one body, one Spirit, one hope, one Lord, one faith, one baptism, and one God and Father of all. Interestingly, the first of these seven *ones* is the one body, suggesting that this is Paul's main focus.

Amid the unity of the body, Paul acknowledges that there is diversity even within this unity. In fact, diversity is needed so that the body reaches its full potential and maturity. Christ has given apostles, prophets, evangelists, and pastor/shepherd-teachers to help equip the body to carry out ministry (4:11–12). The goal is that "we all attain to the unity of the faith" (4:13). But how is it that we possess unity by being part of the one body of Christ but still must strive after unity? Campbell explains, "Those who belong to Christ are now one body—indivisible

24 Campbell, *Paul and Union with Christ,* 293.

and uncorrupted—since the believers' spiritual union with Christ cannot be compromised, and therefore their spiritual union with each other is complete. Nevertheless, our fleshly existence in this world means that the spiritual oneness of the body is expressed through a corrupted and imperfect experience of the church."[25]

Ephesians 4:15–16 contains two references to the body where Christ is the head, and he causes the body to grow in maturity. Believers are to conform themselves to the image of Christ, who is its source of authority and source of growth. Nevertheless, believers are also urged to build themselves up in love since every individual member contributes toward the maturity of the body. And yet ultimately Christ is the one who builds his body. Again, Campbell helpfully summarizes, "the union that believers share with Christ is organic, involving growth that flows from Christ but also into Christ. He is the source of our union and the goal of our union; we come to him and are to become like him. Moreover, the dynamic growth of the body is promoted by Christ *and* involves the contribution of all its members."[26] By their common faith in the Messiah, believers are incorporated into his body and become fellow members who work together to maintain the unity of their faith as they strive toward maturity.

Other Uses

Besides the four categories outlined above, there are other uses of "in Christ," "in the Lord," and "in him/whom" in Ephesians, including instrumental (means), object, cause, and the place where something is revealed. First, several references in 1:3–5 communicate that Christ is the instrument or means to accomplish God's plan:

> Blessed be the God and Father of our Lord Jesus Christ, who has blessed us *in Christ* with every spiritual blessing in the heavenly places, even as he chose us *in him* before the foundation of the

---

25 Campbell, *Paul and Union with Christ*, 281.
26 Campbell, *Paul and Union with Christ*, 282.

world, that we should be holy and blameless before him. In love he predestined us for adoption to himself as sons *through Jesus Christ*, according to the purpose of his will.

Every spiritual blessing is granted to God's people "in Christ" (1:3). Although this use could refer to union with Christ (identification), it is also possible that the phrase modifies "blessed," demonstrating that believers receive the blessings of God *through Jesus Christ* (*dia Iēsou Christou*).[27] Thus God is the agent of blessing, and Christ is the means by which that blessing is bestowed. Paul continues by offering a specific example of God's blessing: he chose us "in him" (1:4) and predestined us "through Jesus Christ" (1:5). Both of these uses demonstrate that Christ is designated as the instrument through whom God's choosing or predestinating adoption occurs. The parallel function of 1:4 and 5 demonstrates that "in him" functions as the means through whom God made his choice as "through Jesus Christ" clearly conveys.[28]

Additional uses of the instrumental use include the following:

For we are his workmanship, created *in Christ Jesus* for good works, which God prepared beforehand, that we should walk in them. (2:10)

This was according to the eternal purpose that he has realized *in Christ Jesus* our Lord, *in whom* we have boldness and access with confidence through our faith in him. (3:11–12)

In these verses we learn that (1) believers were created by God (the agent) through Christ Jesus (the instrument). In other words, believers have their source of life from God, but this work of creation is achieved through the work of Christ. (2) God accomplished his eternal purpose "in Christ Jesus." Again Paul is stating that Christ is

27 See Campbell, *Paul and Union with Christ*, 82–84, 134.
28 See Campbell, *Paul and Union with Christ*, 177, 189, 247, 257.

the instrument or the means through whom God brought about his purpose. Examples of agency are found in 2:18 ("For *through him* we both have access in one Spirit to the Father") and 4:21 ("assuming that you have heard about him and were taught *in him* [or *by him*], as the truth is in Jesus").[29]

Second, in at least three places the "in Christ" language of Ephesians indicates that Jesus is the object of something:

. . . so that we who were the first to hope *in Christ* might be to the praise of his glory. (1:12)

For this reason, because I have heard of your faith *in the Lord Jesus* and your love toward all the saints. (1:15)

. . . that he worked *in Christ* when he raised him from the dead and seated him at his right hand in the heavenly places. (1:20)

In 1:12 Christ is the object of believers' hope, in 1:15 he is the object of their faith, and in 1:20 he is the object that received God's power so that he was raised from the dead.

Third, there are two verses that communicate that Jesus is the cause of something:

I therefore, a prisoner *for the Lord*, urge you to walk in a manner worthy of the calling to which you have been called. (4:1)

Be kind to one another, tenderhearted, forgiving one another, as God *in Christ* forgave you. (4:32)

Paul was a prisoner "in/for the Lord," but this use of the phrase is not communicating union with Christ. Rather, it is conveying the cause

---

29 The difference between *agent* and *instrument* is that *agent* is the direct mover or cause whereas *instrument* is the indirect cause. It is possible that 4:21 should be taken to signify content (*about him*).

of his imprisonment. He was a prisoner because of or for the sake of his commitment to follow and obey Jesus. Also, believers are commanded to forgive others just as God forgave them *in Christ*. Although this use could be understood as indicating instrument (God forgave them *through* Christ), it is best to view it as causal (God forgave them *because of* Christ).[30] Just as God forgave us on account of Christ, so too we should forgive others on account of Christ.

Lastly, there are a few uses where *in Christ* (or its equivalent) conveys the place where something is revealed:

> . . . so that in the coming ages he might show the immeasurable riches of his grace in kindness toward us *in Christ Jesus*. (2:7)

> To him be glory in the church and *in Christ Jesus* throughout all generations, forever and ever. Amen. (3:21)

In 2:7 the kindness of God is revealed toward believers *in Christ Jesus*. That is, God's display of his grace and kindness is evident or manifest in Christ. Furthermore, God's glory is made evident in the church and *in Christ Jesus* to all generations (3:21).[31]

Summary

The frequency of *union with Christ* language in Ephesians demonstrates that it is a central theme in this epistle, especially as it relates to our union, participation, identification, and incorporation with Christ. I, therefore, agree with Campbell when he states that union with Christ is "the essential ingredient that binds all other elements together; it is the webbing that connects the ideas of Paul's web-shaped theological framework. It is for this reason that we can say that every blessing we receive from God is through our union with Christ. It is by being united to him in faith by the Spirit, dying, suffering, rising, and glorying with

30 See Campbell, *Paul and Union with Christ*, 88–89.
31 See Campbell, *Paul and Union with Christ*, 86, 134–37.

him, having been predestined and redeemed in him, being identified with his realm, and being incorporated into his people that believers enjoy the manifold grace of God."[32] Paul's theology cannot be reduced to union with Christ. But union with Christ is often the Christological anchor that grounds his theology and ethic.

---

32 Campbell, *Paul and Union with Christ*, 442.

Walking according to the Spirit

THE GOOD NEWS CANNOT BE GOOD NEWS without first understanding our dire predicament before God saved us. Thus Paul reminds us of the former way that we lived; that is, we walked in sin and death (Eph. 2:1–3, 11–13, 19; 4:17–22). The foundation of walking in the Spirit is what God did for us in Christ (1:11; 4:1). Consequently we have the freedom (desire and ability) now to walk in the Spirit, which generally can be labeled good works (2:10) but also means walking worthy of our calling (4:1), according to the new self (4:23–32), in love (5:1–2), as children of light (5:3–14), with wisdom (5:15–16), filled by the Spirit (5:18–21), and faithfully with the family of God (5:22–6:9).

The Former Way of Walking

The Walking Dead (2:1–3)

The main idea of 2:1–10 is that God graciously works to take people who are dead and makes them alive. In the first three verses, Paul presents the fallen state of all humanity, which is characterized as those who are dead, who follow their fleshly passions and desires, and who are by nature children of wrath. These spiritually dead people, however, are walking (living) a certain way. They are influenced by and live according to the world, the flesh, and the devil. The result is that the walking dead live contrary to God's will and consequently deserve God's coming wrath:

And you were dead in the trespasses and sins in which you once walked, following the course of this world, following the prince of the power of the air, the spirit that is now at work in the sons of disobedience—among whom we all once lived in the passions of our flesh, carrying out the desires of the body and the mind, and were by nature children of wrath, like the rest of mankind. (2:1–3)

Paul declares that prior to faith in Christ, all believers "were dead in the trespasses and sins" (2:1). This reference to the depravity of humanity is true of all who are not reconciled to God through Christ. That is, prior to conversion, all humanity lives in rebellion to God by transgressing his commands and sinning against his revealed will. All humanity is in bondage to sin. In fact, Paul maintains that unsaved people are "dead" in their sins. They are not merely sick or ailing but are spiritually lifeless. They cannot improve their standing before God on their own power. They have neither the desire nor ability to change their status. They need the life-giving power of God to awaken their hearts and minds.

Paul further elaborates that prior to conversion, all humanity walks or lives under the influence of the world, the flesh, and the devil. Before trusting in Christ and receiving the life-giving power of God, our situation is that we follow "the course of this world" (2:2). By "world," Paul is referring to that which is opposed to God, including cultural, social, or political ideologies that are contrary to God and his revealed will. Before knowing Christ, our behavior is essentially determined by the culture and society in which we live. That is, our attitudes, preferences, and habits are formed according to the standard of the world and not according to the principles and power of God (see 1 John 2:15).

Paul adds that not only is humanity dead and under the power of the world, but prior to receiving new life, we follow "the prince of the power of the air" (Eph. 2:2), a clear reference to Satan or the devil. Interestingly, Paul recognizes that the devil is a powerful supernatural being who rules over less powerful evil spirits. The realm of authority of the devil is the "power of the air" (2:2), and the result is that he "is now at work in the sons of disobedience" (2:2). The devil is a spiritual being who is working to destroy humanity. In this passage he is labeled "prince" (or ruler) and a "spirit," and in the Gospels he is called the "prince [or ruler] of demons" (Matt. 9:34; 12:24; Mark 3:22; Luke 11:15) and the "ruler of this world" (John 12:31; 14:30; 16:11). Thus our former way of life was under the influence and authority of the devil and his minions who are active in the world today. Satan is called "the ruler of this world" (John 12:31) and "the god of this world" (2 Cor. 4:4) who blinds unbelievers from seeing the truth. He takes advantage of believers when they sin (Eph. 4:27), sets traps or snares for the unwary (1 Tim. 3:7; 2 Tim. 2:26), and prowls around like a roaring lion seeking to devour the unprepared (1 Pet. 5:8). In fact, "the whole world lies in the power of the evil one" (1 John 5:19).

Finally, Paul indicates that the problem is not merely external, because there is an internal foe: the flesh. Every person is affected by the fall and suffers under the devastating effects of sin. By "flesh," Paul is referring to our fallen, corrupted human nature and not simply the physical body. Our natural propensity is to spurn God and his law. We are influenced by our fleshly passions, which cause us to follow the "desires of the body and the mind" (Eph. 2:3). Thus "by nature" or by birth (see Gal. 2:15) we are all children who deserved God's wrath. Thankfully, this is not the end of the story nor the end of the passage. The lavish grace of God intrudes into the deadness of humanity causing new life.

Alienated Strangers (2:11–13)

Not only is all humanity dead in sins apart from the life-giving power of God, but Gentiles were in a state of alienation. That is, we were *separated, alienated, strangers, hopeless, godless,* and *far* from God.

> Therefore remember that at one time you Gentiles in the flesh, called "the uncircumcision" by what is called the circumcision, which is made in the flesh by hands—remember that you were at that time separated from Christ, alienated from the commonwealth of Israel and strangers to the covenants of promise, having no hope and without God in the world. But now in Christ Jesus you who once were far off have been brought near by the blood of Christ. (2:11–13)

Paul exhorts his readers to remember their former situation before they received the grace of God through the work of Christ. Indeed, their (and our) situation was bleak. Paul identifies his target audience as "Gentiles in the flesh" and those called "the uncircumcision" by the circumcision or his Jewish audience (2:11). Such Gentiles did not have the covenant sign of circumcision, and they thus were estranged or separated from God. Specifically, Gentiles are labeled with six deficiencies that summarize their preconversion state. As the covenant people of God, the people of Israel possessed undeserved blessings from God (see Rom. 3:2; 9:4–5).

First, the Gentiles were previously "separated from Christ" (Eph. 2:12). This deficiency highlights the central problem and is probably why Paul mentions it first. After all, every spiritual blessing (1:3–14) is obtainable from God only through Christ and for those united to him. Furthermore, if our liberation from the world, the flesh, and the devil comes from being united with Christ, then to be without Christ is to be without the power to overcome these forces and still be under their dominion and under the wrath of God. Second, we were "alienated from the commonwealth of Israel" (2:12). As Gentiles, we were estranged from the chosen people of God and all the privileges of those who could claim citizenship in Israel. Later in this passage, Paul writes that those who are in Christ "are no longer strangers and aliens" but "are fellow citizens with the saints and members of the household of God" (2:19). Because of the reconciliation secured by Christ's atonement, Gentiles who were once strangers become fellow citizens in God's kingdom with a heavenly homeland (see Phil. 3:20). Third, Gentiles were "strangers to the covenants of promise" (Eph. 2:12). God ratified several covenants in the Old Testament with Israel, including the Abrahamic, the Mosaic, the Davidic, and the new covenant.[1] These covenants included the blessings of God and the promise of a future deliverer or Messiah.

---

1   See, e.g., Gen. 12:1–4; 15:8–18; 17:1–14 (Abrahamic covenant); Ex. 24:1–8 (Mosaic covenant); 2 Sam. 7:12–17; 23:5 (Davidic covenant); and Jer. 31:31–34; 32:38–40; Ezek. 36:23–36 (new covenant).

Fourth, they had "no hope" (2:12) of true salvation, reconciliation with God, or future resurrection with Christ. Fifth, they were "without God in the world" (2:12). Ironically, most Gentiles believed in a plethora of gods and so this critique might have been roundly rejected (see 1 Cor. 8:5–6; Gal. 4:8). Paul's point, however, is that even though they affirmed and worshiped these gods, they had no relationship with the true and living God—the God who created the heavens and the earth, the God who predestined a people for himself, the God who provided a way of reconciliation through his own Son, and the God who saves and seals those who are united to his Son by faith. Finally, Gentiles who are without Christ are characterized as "far off" (Eph. 2:13). Several texts in the Old Testament describe Gentile nations as being "far," whereas Israel is designated as "near."[2] As Paul will go on to explain, this once desperate plight of the Gentiles has changed since "by the blood of Christ" many have been brought near (2:13). Apart from Christ, however, we are separated and alienated from God.

Futile Minds and Hardened Hearts (4:17–22)

The final text to consider that describes a person's pre-Christ state is found in 4:17–22. Paul maintains that non-Christians live according to the "futility of their minds" (4:17); they are "darkened in their understanding" (4:18), ignorant (4:18), have hard hearts (4:18), and are "callous" (4:19). Such degenerate thinking naturally leads to immoral and depraved living where people succumb to sensuality, impurity (4:19), and deceitful desires (4:22):

> Now this I say and testify in the Lord, that you must no longer walk as the Gentiles do, in the futility of their minds. They are darkened in their understanding, alienated from the life of God because of the ignorance that is in them, due to their hardness of heart. They have become callous and have given themselves up to sensuality, greedy

---

2   See Deut. 28:49; 29:22; 1 Kings 8:41; Isa. 5:26; Jer. 5:15; also see Acts 2:39; 22:21; cf. Ps. 148:14.

to practice every kind of impurity. . . . Put off your old self, which belongs to your former manner of life and is corrupt through deceitful desires. (4:17–19, 22)

After discussing the unity and diversity of the body of Christ that will lead the church to maturity, Paul exhorts his audience not (or no longer) to live as pagan, unbelieving Gentiles but as those who have renewed minds and transformed hearts. He thus resumes the appeal of 4:1, where he implored them to "walk in a manner worthy" of their calling. The seriousness and solemnity of Paul's exhortation is conveyed through the additional verb "testify" and the prepositional phrase "in the Lord," which communicates the source of his authority (4:17). Although they are Gentiles, Paul urges his readers not to live ("walk") as Gentiles since they are now children of God. First, they should not walk "in the futility of their minds" (4:17). Faithful living always starts with right thinking. In Romans, Paul mentions those who acknowledged God but did not honor or give thanks to him, so they "became futile in their thinking" (Rom. 1:21). Second, as unregenerate Gentiles, they were "darkened in their understanding" (Eph. 4:18). In contrast, believers are those whose hearts are enlightened (1:18). Third, unbelieving Gentiles are "alienated from the life of God" (4:18). Earlier, Paul reminded his Gentile audience that they were "alienated from the commonwealth of Israel" (2:12), but this time he says they were estranged from the life that comes from God. Without God's life-giving Spirit, they were dead in their trespasses and sins (2:1, 5).

Fourth, they had hard hearts (4:18) and so were obstinate and insensible. Bruce defines the hardening of their hearts as "the progressive inability of conscience to convict them of wrongdoing."[3] Fifth, they "have become callous" (4:19). This verb is only used here in the New Testament and means "to lose the capacity to feel shame or embarrassment."[4] Sixth, their calloused hearts and minds have led "to sensuality" and "every

---

3   F. F. Bruce, *Colossians, Philemon, Ephesians*, NICNT (Grand Rapids, MI: Eerdmans, 1984), 355.

4   L&N 25.197.

kind of impurity" (4:19). *Sensuality* refers to the "lack of self-constraint that involves one in conduct that violates all bounds of what is socially acceptable,"[5] and "it is probably best understood as undisciplined behavior especially, though not exclusively, of a sexual nature."[6] *Impurity* refers to unrestrained sexual and other deviant behavior. Finally, they are characterized by embracing "deceitful desires" (4:22) or sinful passions that corrupt and destroy someone. These desires oppose God and his gospel. Again, this description, though realistic, is grim. Without the grace and mercy of God, the natural person remains under the wrath of God.

The Foundation for Walking in the Spirit

In language, certain words are sometimes seen as "throw away" words, including conjunctions. After all, they are words that *conjoin* or *join* other words. They are merely the glue that holds the important pieces together. But such a view of conjunctions is shortsighted since these (usually small) words often provide the rationale or logic of how one portion of a discourse relates to another. In Ephesians, Paul desires his readers to walk according to the Spirit. That is, he wants Christians to be filled with and influenced by the Spirit so that they live according to God's revealed will (5:18). But Paul's exhortations for believers do not appear randomly in Ephesians (or in any of his letters). Rather, they are built atop the foundation laid out earlier in the letter. Thus the commands that Paul relates to his audience are based upon the reality of a previous life transformation.

We love because God first loved us (1 John 4:19). We obey because God first moved in our hearts and gives us the ability and desire to follow his commands (Phil. 2:12–13). The commands or imperatives in Ephesians are always built upon the reality that God has already done a work in our lives through the gospel of Jesus Christ. Or, as some biblical scholars explain it, the indicative (what God has done for us in Christ) always precedes the imperative (our response of obedience to

---

5 BDAG 141.

6 E. Best, *Ephesians*, ICC (London: T&T Clark, 1998), 422.

God's commands). To get this order wrong is to get the gospel wrong. A salvation of works says, "Do this and live," but the gospel says, "God has done this, now live." This distinction is precisely where conjunctions come in. Two significant conjunctions in Ephesians that communicate the significance of this gospel-clarifying reality are *but* (Greek: *de*) and *therefore* (Greek: *oun*).

"But . . ." (2:4, 13)

In Ephesians 2 Paul details the spiritual situation of fallen humanity apart from God's intervening grace. Humanity is not spiritually sick but spiritually dead. The consequences of following the world, the flesh, and the devil result in being labeled "children of wrath" (2:3) and "sons of disobedience" (2:2). The remedy for this dire description, however, is not obedience to God and his commands. Such a feat is impossible for those who are spiritually dead and therefore lack the ability or desire to do so. Instead, the remedy begins with God: "But God . . . made us alive together with Christ" (2:4–5). Before we can obey God's commands, we must experience new life. And the only way that a person is regenerated and made alive is through the intervening grace of God. We were dead in our trespasses and sins . . . but God. We followed the ways of the world, the flesh, and the devil . . . but God. We were sons of disobedience and children of wrath . . . but God. Before people obey the will of God, they must first be made alive by the power of God found in the gospel.

Another use of *but* (*de*) that demonstrates the reversal needed for obedience is found in 2:13. In the context, Paul describes lost Gentiles as being separated from Christ, alienated from Israel, strangers to the covenants, without hope and without God, and therefore far from God. He then adds, "But now in Christ Jesus you . . . have been brought near by the blood of Christ" (2:13). Here we see a radical shift that is reminiscent of that found in 2:4. It is only through the gospel and our union with Christ that our status is changed. We were once far off but now have been brought near. More specifically, Paul indicates that the Gentile inclusion into the people of God is "by the blood of Christ." That is, it is through the sacrificial death of Christ (see 1:7). Our status is not changed by obedience to God's directives. Rather, our status is changed only through the supernatural work of God in the gospel of Christ.

"Therefore . . ." (4:1)

A second conjunction that demonstrates the proper foundation of good works is *therefore* (*oun*). In 4:1 Paul turns from focusing on the indicatives of what God has done for us in Christ to our response based on our new status. He writes, "I therefore . . . urge you to walk in a manner worthy of the calling to which you have been called." The word *therefore* grounds Paul's imperatives in the indicatives of the previous three chapters. Up to this point, Paul has only used one imperative. In 2:11 he exhorts his readers to "remember" their previous condition when they were far from God, his covenants, and his promises. In chapters 4–6, however, Paul uses thirty-nine imperatives. But again, the order here is what is crucial to grasp.

Being a Christian is not primarily about living a certain way or about obeying certain commands or about not breaking God's rules. Rather, being a Christian is first and foremost about having been made alive by the power of God. "Being" precedes "doing." Before we *do* or *don't do* certain things, we must first *become* a new creation in Christ. Our own effort to clean up our lives or to try harder to please God is merely moralism. The gospel message is that we will never be good enough and that no amount of good works can save us. In 4:1 Paul calls Christians to walk worthy of their calling. Yes, Christians should strive to please God through their actions. But the foundation of these actions must be built upon one who has already trusted in Christ, having been made alive by the power of God. There is no freedom to walk according to the commands of God if someone does not first have the life-giving power of the Spirit of God.

The Freedom of Walking in the Spirit

The term *walking* (Greek: *peripateō*) occurs thirty-two times in Paul's writings, always used metaphorically for a person's lifestyle. That is, the term relates to how people live or conduct their lives. In Ephesians,

Paul uses this term eight times, the highest number of uses in any of his letters (25 percent of all occurrences). Paul, therefore, places a high value on how Christians behave. It is part of the warp and woof of what it means to be a follower of Christ.

In the first half of Ephesians (chapters 1–3), Paul uses the term *walk* only twice, and never as a command. He indicates that before believers were made alive in Christ, they were dead in the sins in which they "once walked" (2:2), resulting in following the world, the flesh (sinful nature), and the devil. But now that believers have been raised from the dead and are reigning with Christ, as God's workmanship created for good works, God's purpose for them is to "walk" in the good works that God has prepared beforehand (2:10).

In the second half of the letter (chapters 4–6), Paul emphasizes the need for Christians to live according to God's revealed will. Five times he commands Christians to walk a certain way:

I . . . urge you to *walk* in a manner worthy of the calling to which you have been called, with all humility and gentleness, with patience, bearing with one another in love, eager to maintain the unity of the Spirit in the bond of peace. (4:1–3)

You must no longer *walk* as the Gentiles [*walk*], in the futility of their minds. (4:17)

And *walk* in love, as Christ loved us and gave himself up for us, a fragrant offering and sacrifice to God. (5:2)

For at one time you were darkness, but now you are light in the Lord. *Walk* as children of light. (5:8)

Look carefully then how you *walk*, not as unwise but as wise. (5:15)

The key, however, is that our union with Christ is both the foundation and the fuel for Christian living. First, union with Christ is the foundation because previously we were spiritually dead as those who were "in Adam," our representative head. But now that we are "in Christ" every spiritual blessing is ours (1:3), including the Holy Spirit himself (1:13; 4:30). Second, union with Christ is the fuel of Christian living. Because the old person has been crucified with Christ, we are able "to put on the new self, created after the likeness of God in true righteousness and holiness" (4:24). Both the ability and desire to walk in good works flow from our union with Christ, which is established by faith.

We must clearly understand the order in which Paul presents union with Christ and walking in the Spirit. To reverse the order of these is to distort the gospel. We do not live according to God's commands in order to gain favor from God. Rather, because we have received the blessings secured through our union with Christ, we can now walk in newness of life.

Walking in Good Works (2:10)

The fact that good works are not the foundation of our relationship with God does not mean that good works are not important. After describing unregenerate humanity as those who walk in their trespasses and sins (2:1–3), Paul concludes the section by stating that believers are those who are called to "walk" in good works that God has prepared for them (2:10). By using the verb *walk*, Paul connects 2:10 to the beginning of the chapter. In 2:1–2 Paul painted the bleak picture of humanity as those who *walked* in rebellion to God. But later, using the same verb, he indicates that those who are made alive as part of God's re-creation are called to *walk* according to the good works preordained by God. Paul is clear that our works do not save us nor do they provide us any reason to boast before God. We are saved by grace through faith. It is "not your own doing" (2:8). It is "the gift of God" (2:8). It is "not a result of works" (2:9). And yet believers have been summoned to walk in the good works that God has prepared for us. They are not what saves us. But, having been saved, they are what sets us apart as God's people.

Walking Worthy of Our Calling (4:1)

As Paul transitions from the doctrinal or theological section of his letter (chapters 1–3), to the application or practical section of his letter (chapters 4–6), he signals this transition by the word *therefore*. He then offers the main focus of what the rest of the letter will involve. He states, "I . . . urge you to walk" (4:1). Paul, as an apostle of Christ and a prisoner on his behalf, urges his readers to live a certain way. Thus it is incumbent on Christians to strive fervently to obey God's word and God's will. More specifically, Paul implores his readers "to walk in a manner worthy of the calling" (4:1) to which they were called. Thus believers have an obligation to conduct their lives based on the calling they have received from God.

Christians often speak about being "called" by God, often implying that they should follow a certain profession, live in a certain location, or pursue a certain direction in their lives. Interestingly, however, when the New Testament speaks of calling, it rarely speaks of a vocation or a location,[7] but of one's character. Consider the following verses:

> For you were called to freedom, brothers. Only do not use your freedom as an opportunity for the flesh, but through love serve one another. (Gal. 5:13)

> For God has not called us for impurity, but in holiness. (1 Thess. 4:7)

> For to this you have been called, because Christ also suffered for you, leaving you an example, so that you might follow in his steps. (1 Pet. 2:21)

---

7   Possible exceptions are found in Acts 13:2, where Paul and Barnabas are set apart "for the work to which [the Holy Spirit has] called them," and Acts 16:10, where Paul sees a vision of a Macedonian man urging him to come to Macedonia to help them. Paul and the others concluded, "God had called us to preach the gospel to them." Of course, these are descriptive verses and should not be interpreted as normative for all Christians. On the other hand, all Christians are called to display godly character.

Do not repay evil for evil or reviling for reviling, but on the contrary, bless, for to this you were called, that you may obtain a blessing. (1 Pet. 3:9)

We believers are called to the freedom of serving others, to holiness, to suffer as Christ suffered, and to bless those who revile us. Or, as Paul puts it here in Ephesians, we are called to walk worthy of our calling, which in the context relates specially to living in unity with other believers and using our gifts to build up the church. But, to stress this point once again, our behavior is always subsequent to our being born anew by the power of God. Our conduct always follows our calling. It is only once we have received new life and are indwelt by the Spirit of God that we are able to follow the commands of God faithfully and worthily. The repetition of the idea of calling ("the *calling* to which you have been *called*") highlights its importance. Christians have been called by God to follow his will and thus live worthily of that calling.

Walking according to the New Self (4:23–32)

In Ephesians 4:17–22 Paul urged his readers to "no longer walk as the Gentiles do, in the futility of their minds" (4:17) since those who are unregenerate are "darkened in their understanding" and have hard hearts (4:18–19), which leads to immorality, sensuality, and impurity (4:19, 22). Instead, those who are united to Christ are those who have renewed minds (4:23). Before people can truly walk according to God's will, their minds need to be renewed and transformed. This renewal is a work of God's Spirit (Titus 3:5), and it is also something that believers are commanded to seek (see also Rom. 12:2). Paul further commands believers "to put on the new self" (Eph. 4:24). Christians are never merely to put aside or flee from sin; they are also to put on or pursue righteousness.[8] The "new self" that believers are to put on includes a new mindset and lifestyle that are "created after the likeness of God"

---

8   See Rom. 13:12, 14; Gal. 3:27; Eph. 6:11, 14; Col. 3:10, 12; 1 Thess. 5:8; 1 Tim. 6:11; 2 Tim. 2:22.

(4:24), which indicates that God is both the author of life and the very pattern of life itself (cf. Col. 3:10). Paul further clarifies that the new self is created "in true righteousness and holiness" (Eph. 4:24). Thus the goal of a renewed mind is a renewed lifestyle—a lifestyle that seeks righteousness and holiness in order to be conformed to the image of Christ. But this changed reality does not negate the need for Christians to fight to become what they are. It is not enough to claim a new status without pursuing the fruit that such a status leads to. So although it is true that because of our union with Christ we are new creations, we still must seek to forsake the old self and embrace the new self. In other words, our renewed thinking should always lead to righteous and holy living.

Paul continues by providing specific directives for his readers. Those who have renewed minds and have put on the new self must live a certain way (often given as a prohibition followed by a command). First, they are not to lie but to speak the truth (4:25). That is, they are to "put away falsehood" (cf. Col. 3:9) and instead "let each one of you speak the truth" (cf. Zech. 8:16). It is likely that Paul's reference to "neighbor" here in Ephesians 4:25 specifically refers to other believers, which is confirmed by his reasoning: "for we are members one of another." It is not enough to merely stop lying; believers are also called to positively speak the truth.

Second, believers are called to "be angry and . . . not sin" (4:26). This phrase is an exact quote from Psalm 4:4 (4:5 LXX). Paul's meaning is that Christians should occasionally be roused to anger if the circumstances demand it, not that they should be characterized by anger (cf. Eph. 4:31). We know it is possible to be angry without sinning since Jesus was angry (Mark 3:5) but was without sin. And yet the following commands ("Do not sin," "Do not let the sun go down on your anger") remind readers that it is not easy for people to be angry without sin (cf. James 1:19–20). Therefore, it is crucial for believers to deal with anger immediately so that it does not fester and lead to sin. If we fail to deal with sin, we end up giving "opportunity to the devil" (Eph. 4:27). The devil does not produce the anger, but he may exploit it if it remains unchecked.

Third, Paul urges those who put on the new self not to steal but to work hard so that they can help others in need (4:28). Stealing is forbidden in the Old Testament (Ex. 20:15) and the New Testament (Matt. 19:18). Some were apparently stealing from their employers or from others, and so Paul commands them to "no longer steal." The remedy is to be willing to work hard so that they "have something to share with anyone in need" (Eph. 4:28). Such was the pattern of the early church and something that was expected of all Christians (Acts 20:35; 1 John 3:17). The antidote for stealing is generosity.

Fourth, believers are not to speak what is harmful but what builds up (Eph. 4:29). In the space of a few verses, Paul again returns to the importance of speech (cf. 4:25). Paul states, "Let no corrupting talk come out of your mouths." The term *corrupt* (*sapros*) can refer to something rotten, spoiled, or putrid. In the Gospels, it describes "diseased" trees (Matt. 7:17–18), "bad" fruit (Matt. 7:17–18), or "bad" fish (Matt. 13:48). Here in Ephesians 4:29, the term refers to that which tears down instead of building up, a central concern of Paul in this chapter (cf. 4:12, 16). Consequently, believers must make every effort to use their words to build up or edify others and not to use their words to tear others down. Such conversation displays the grace of God to others when others are encouraged by carefully chosen words.

Fifth, someone who has put on the new self is someone who does not grieve the Holy Spirit (4:30). Because of the connection of this verse with the previous verse (see the *and* at the beginning of the verse), one way the Holy Spirit is grieved is when Christians speak unkindly to (or about) each other. Thus when God's people are maligned, God's Spirit is grieved, demonstrating the solidarity between God's people and God's Spirit. Because the Holy Spirit can be grieved, Paul thus understands the Spirit in fully personal terms. That is, the Spirit is understood as a person with feelings and emotions and is not simply a power or a force. Indeed, the Spirit is the third person of the Trinity and is the one who seals Christians "for the day of redemption."

Finally, Paul exhorts his readers not to be bitter or angry but to forgive one another (4:31–32). They are to put various sins to death including bitterness, wrath, anger, clamor, and slander since they are contrary to the Spirit's work of regeneration and threaten unity among God's people. In contrast, believers are urged to "be kind to one another, tenderhearted, forgiving one another" (4:32; cf. Col. 3:12–13). Kindness is an attribute of God and one that he displays to his people. Paul thus encourages Christians to imitate God. Tenderheartedness refers to displaying compassion to others (cf. 1 Pet. 3:8). The last exhortation is to forgive "as God in Christ forgave you" (cf. Col. 3:13). Just as believers have freely received grace from God through the work of Christ, so too they are to freely forgive others when wronged. In this section, Paul unleashes thirteen imperatives (commands and prohibitions) demonstrating what it means to put off the old self and put on the new self.

Walking in Love (5:1–2)

Part of what it means to live as a new creation is to imitate the one who created us and re-created us anew. Thus Paul urges believers to imitate God by walking in love. Although these verses begin a new chapter, the contents of Ephesians 5:1–2 are closely tied to the preceding context as is indicated by the word "Therefore" (5:1). Elsewhere Paul exhorts his readers to imitate other churches (1 Thess. 2:14), himself (1 Cor. 4:16), or Christ (1 Thess. 1:6), but only here does he call for believers to "be imitators of God" (Eph. 5:1). Paul reminds his readers that they are "beloved children," the basis upon which they are to imitate God. As we experience the love of God as those who are adopted into his family (1:5), we are empowered and motivated to love others. As Lincoln notes, "Believers have been adopted into God's family (cf. 1:5) and should exhibit the family resemblance."[9]

Paul then expands on the command to imitate God by specifically enjoining Christians to "walk in love" (5:2). In other words, the way in which we imitate God is by walking in love. This is the third time Paul has specifically commanded his readers to walk a certain way (4:1, 17; see also 5:8, 15). In this case, believers are to live as those who have a

---

9   Andrew D. Lincoln, *Ephesians*, WBC 42 (Dallas: Word, 1990), 310.

genuine love for others. The perfect illustration of such love is found in the life of Christ. He is the one who "loved us and gave himself up for us" (5:2). But his example not only illustrates what love is; it also provides the motivation for believers' love. We love *as* he loves and *because* of his love for us. Not only did the Father give his Son, but the Son freely surrendered his life (he "gave himself") as an offering for others (see John 10:11–18; 15:13). Jesus took the initiative to willingly lay down his life for the benefit of others and in the place of others.[10] He bore the wrath of God, becoming a "fragrant offering and sacrifice" that was accepted by God to make atonement for sin. God's children are therefore expected to follow him by loving others even as Christ loved by giving of himself. This command to love can be seen as the highest of virtues because if love is displayed, the other virtues will naturally be practiced. When Christians love each other, they will speak the truth, they will not sin when they are angry, they will share with others, they will build others up with their words, and they will be kind and forgive one another.

Walking as Children of Light (5:3–14)

In this passage, we have the fourth explicit instance of Paul exhorting his readers to walk a certain way. Here they are urged to "walk as children of light" (Eph. 5:8). Light has ethical connotations, and so the implication is that believers should avoid sinful behavior (darkness) and live righteous and holy lives (light). In the first section of this passage (5:3–6), Paul admonishes Christians to avoid the sins of sexual immorality, impurity, and greed (or covetousness). Such sins are not fitting for Christians, so Paul states that these sins "must not even be named among you" since it is not "proper among saints" (5:3). Earlier he wrote that God chose them to be holy and blameless (1:4), so their behavior should be consistent with their new identity as God's chosen people who have been given a holy calling (4:1). They must also avoid "filthiness," "foolish talk," and "crude joking" (5:4) but instead be characterized by thanksgiving. Those who are characterized by such

---

10 See also 5:25; 2 Cor. 5:14, 21; Gal. 1:4; 3:13; 1 Tim. 2:6; Titus 2:14.

darkness have "no inheritance in the kingdom of Christ and God" (5:5). Furthermore, he warns that those who willfully practice such sins are in danger of experiencing "the wrath of God" (5:6).

In 5:3–6, Paul lists various sins that believers are to avoid, and beginning in 5:7 he offers reasons why they should not associate with the ungodly lifestyle of unbelievers. Believers should not be "partners" with them, meaning they should not embrace any false teaching and the deviant lifestyle associated with such teaching. As Thielman notes, "Paul's point here is that fully participating in the worldview and conduct of unbelievers in matters of sex and money is incompatible with membership in the people of God."[11] Instead of imitating the world, they should imitate God (5:1). The rationale that Paul provides is simple: their identity has changed. They were "at one time" darkness "but now" they are light (5:8). That is, before they were redeemed, sealed with the Spirit, and given a new nature, they were in a state of moral and spiritual darkness. And Paul does not merely state that they were *in* darkness but that they *were* darkness. By nature they were that which is opposed to God. But now they are light and are to "walk as children of light" (5:8). Thus believers are commanded to become what they already are. Their lifestyle should conform to the reality of who they are as new creations in Christ. Again, the order here is crucial. Because of who we already are based on our union with Christ (indicative), we are exhorted to live a certain way (imperative). A good tree will produce good fruit and a tree of light will produce the "fruit of light" (5:9). Such "fruit" is the result of having already received new life in Christ and the life-giving power of God. It is the result and by-product of having faith in Christ and not the prerequisite for being accepted by God. Apart from the life-giving work of the Spirit, believers have no power or desire to overcome sin. But because believers have been given a new nature, their desires and abilities are changed and transformed.

Paul offers specific examples of what it means to "walk as children of light" (5:8), including the need "to discern what is pleasing to the Lord"

---

11   Frank Thielman, *Ephesians*, BECNT (Grand Rapids, MI: Baker, 2010), 335–36.

(5:10) and to avoid and expose unfruitful works of darkness (5:11). As believers, we have the duty to expose the deeds of darkness of those believers who have gone astray so that they will be convicted of their error and return to their senses. In 1 Corinthians 5:13 Paul instructs the church to expose or judge the person who had inappropriate sexual relations, saying, "Purge the evil person from among you" (cf. 1 Tim. 5:20; 2 Tim. 4:2; Titus 1:9, 13; 2:15). One of the functions of light is to expose and illuminate the darkness.

Walking with Wisdom and Understanding (5:15–17)

In this passage, Paul exhorts his readers to walk with wisdom and understanding. He begins with a command to "look carefully" (Eph. 5:15), which emphasizes the importance and urgency of this admonition. Paul then unpacks this command with a pair of contrasts. First, we are to walk "not as unwise but as wise" (5:15). In chapter 1 Paul prayed that God would give his readers "the Spirit of wisdom and of revelation" (1:17). In Proverbs we read, "The fear of the LORD is the beginning of wisdom" (Prov. 9:10; cf. Prov. 1:7; 15:33). Knowledge of and reverence for the Creator of all things and his ways are the foundation of true wisdom. Here in Ephesians 5, he exhorts them to live according to the understanding gained from insight into God's will and God's workings. Lincoln explains, "To live as a wise person is not just to have knowledge but to have skill in living, to have the sort of perception that authenticates itself in practice."[12]

In particular, Christians are to walk wisely by "making the best use of the time" (5:16; cf. Col. 4:5). That is, we should take full advantage of every opportunity that is presented to us and use those opportunities to advance God's kingdom. It is not sufficient to play it safe and avoid evil. Believers must actively seek to employ the gifts and grace we have received to push back the darkness and walk as children of light. Paul then provides the rationale for his admonition: "because the days are evil" (Eph. 5:16). This statement provides insight into Paul's

---

12 Lincoln, *Ephesians*, 341.

eschatology (see chapter 5 in this volume). If the days are now evil, the time is coming when the Messiah will come and make all things right. For now, however, we are exhorted to live wisely, seeking to redeem the time we now have.

The second contrast that Paul urges is to "not be foolish, but understand what the will of the Lord is" (5:17). Foolishness is similar to being "unwise" (5:15), and the Old Testament is replete with warnings to avoid such behavior (see Prov. 10:23; 23:9; 24:7). Here, the Lord's will refers to God's moral purpose for humanity. Thus believers are encouraged to discover and understand what God has revealed in his word regarding his desire for how Christians are to live. The concept of *understanding* "goes beyond simple cognitive awareness to applied knowledge."[13] Because believers have already "learned Christ" (Eph. 4:20) and now have become "light in the Lord" (5:8), they should seek to do what is "pleasing to the Lord" (5:10) by actively pursuing and living out his will.

Walking Filled by the Spirit (5:18–21)

Paul also exhorts his readers to walk being filled by (or with) the Spirit. Negatively, they are to "not get drunk with wine" (5:18). Drunkenness was not only a common problem in the first century;[14] it was also sometimes integrated into pagan worship. For example, the cult of Dionysus (or Bacchus) used the vine as its cultic symbol, emphasizing that which it treasured. One of the problems with drunkenness is that it leads to "debauchery," a "behavior which shows lack of concern or thought for the consequences of an action."[15] Instead of becoming drunk and under the influence of alcohol, Paul positively commands that Christians "be filled with the Spirit" (5:18). The phrase "filled with the Spirit" could be understood in two ways. First, the Spirit could refer to the *content* of that with which Christians are filled ("filled *with* the Spirit"). The other

---

13 Clinton E. Arnold, *Ephesians*, ZECNT (Grand Rapids, MI: Zondervan, 2010), 347.

14 For other admonitions against drunkenness in Paul's writings, see Rom. 13:13; 1 Cor. 5:11; 6:10; 1 Thess. 5:7–8; 1 Tim. 3:8; Titus 2:3 (cf. Matt. 24:49; Luke 12:45; 1 Pet. 4:3).

15 L&N 88.96.

option refers to the *means* by which Christians are filled ("filled *by* the Spirit"). Although most English translations opt for the former interpretation, the latter option is legitimate since it parallels the previous statement (getting drunk with wine refers to the means by which someone gets drunk).[16] If such is the case, then perhaps the content of what Christians are to be filled with is the fullness of the triune God (3:19).

The main idea of 5:18 is being filled with/by the Spirit. Verses 19–21 then provide the results of what it looks like when someone is filled by/with the Spirit, which is signaled in the Greek by a series of five adverbial participles (addressing, singing and making melody, giving thanks, and submitting).[17] That is, Spirit-filled individuals (1) sing to each other, (2) sing to the Lord, (3) continually give thanks for everything to God, and (4) submit to one another. First, Spirit-filled believers address "one another in psalms and hymns and spiritual songs" (5:19; cf. Col. 3:16). Interestingly, Paul highlights the horizontal dimension of singing. When believers truly sing to God, they are also addressing and encouraging one another. Second, Spirit-filled believers sing and make "melody to the Lord" with their hearts (Eph. 5:19). The focus here is on the vertical or God-ward dimension of singing. Such singing probably involves the same act as the previous one with a different emphasis. Pliny, the governor of Bithynia in Asia Minor, described Christians as worshiping and singing to Jesus. He stated that they "regularly assembled on a certain day before daybreak. They recited a hymn antiphonally to Christ as (their) God."[18]

Third, Spirit-filled believers give "thanks always and for everything to God the Father in the name of our Lord Jesus Christ" (5:20). Paul supplies four modifiers that clarify his meaning. Christians are to give thanks "always," specifying that this should be a regular or constant

16 See the CSB ("And don't get drunk with wine, which leads to reckless actions, but be filled by the Spirit") and the NET ("And do not get drunk with wine, which is debauchery, but be filled by the Spirit").

17 Although there are five participles, there are only four distinct elements since singing and making melody are linked together grammatically.

18 Pliny the Younger, *Letters*, 10.96. Cited from Craig A. Evans, *Ancient Texts for New Testament Studies: A Guide to Background Literature* (Peabody, MA: Hendrickson, 2005), 299.

part of a believer's life (cf. 1 Thess. 5:18). They are to give thanks "for everything," including trials and suffering. They are to give thanks "to God the Father" because he is the Creator and sustainer of all things. Finally, they are to give thanks "in the name of our Lord Jesus Christ" because he is the risen Lord and the one who intercedes on behalf of his people. Finally, Spirit-filled believers submit "to one another out of reverence for Christ" (Eph. 5:21). Based on the context, Paul is most likely referring to the various social relationships that follow: wives submitting to their husbands; children to parents; and slaves to masters. That which should motivate a Christian to submit is awe-filled "reverence for Christ." The presence of the Spirit in believers is essential to walking according to the ethical injunctions that Paul provides in the second half of Ephesians.

Walking Faithfully with the Family of God (5:22–6:9)

Finally, to live as a new creation in Christ means walking faithfully as part of the family of God. This includes: (1) wives submitting to their husbands and husbands loving their wives as Christ loves the church (5:22–33); (2) children obeying and honoring their parents and parents not provoking but bringing their children up in the fear and admonition of the Lord (6:1–4); and (3) slaves obeying their masters and masters stopping threatening their slaves, and treating them without partiality (6:5–9). Being part of the family of God affects all of our domestic relationships.

Marriage is an institution created by God. But the covenant between a husband and wife is modeled after the relationship of Christ's love for the church. Just as Christ loves, sanctifies, cleanses, nourishes, and cherishes his bride, so also husbands should treat their brides in the same way. Wives are exhorted to submit to and respect their husbands (5:22, 24, 33; cf. Col. 3:18; Titus 2:5; 1 Pet. 3:1, 5). That is, wives are urged to willingly or voluntarily yield to the leadership of their own husbands as to the Lord. Submission in no way suggests that women are inferior to men but only that they have different God-ordained roles. Husbands are exhorted to love their own wives (Eph. 5:25, 28, 33). They are to love their wives unconditionally as Christ loved the church even when she was unfaithful and unworthy. They are to love their wives sacrificially, willing to give up their rights and interests just as Christ gave himself up for the church. They are to love their wives purposefully, just as Christ sanctifies, cleanses, and presents his bride as pure. And they are to love their wives affectionately, providing for them as Christ nourishes and cherishes the church.

But not only is the marriage relationship impacted by the gospel; the parent-child relationship is likewise impacted. Children are to obey their parents "in the Lord" (6:1), which entails obedience that results from a commitment to Christ as Lord. Similarly, fathers are instructed to train their children in the ways of the Lord (6:4). Children are to obey and honor their parents because it is right (6:1), because it is commanded by God (6:2), and because there is a reward (6:3). Paul singles out fathers, which underscores their leadership in the family. Fathers should take their role of helping to educate and train their children seriously.

Finally, note the Christological emphasis found in the relationship between slaves and masters: as slaves of Christ (6:6), slaves are to obey their masters as if they were obeying or serving Christ (6:5, 7) since they will be rewarded by Christ (6:8). Masters should treat their slaves with respect ("do the same to them") because they too have a heavenly Lord/Master (6:9). Paul did not explicitly condone or condemn slavery in this passage, but (or because) his intent was to address how God's people ought to behave in the midst of such reality. Paul addressed other concerns about slavery elsewhere.[19] Here he provides instructions from a biblical worldview as to how Christian slaves and masters should function in a way that is honoring to God.

Summary

Before people repent and believe in the finished work of Christ, they are spiritually dead in their sins, alienated from God, and possess

---

19 See 1 Cor. 7:21–22; 12:13; Gal. 3:28; Col. 3:11, 22; 4:1; 1 Tim. 6:1–2; Titus 2:9–10; Philem. 15–16.

minds and hearts that are carnal and depraved. The pivotal change in a person's life comes from the resurrecting power of God and not from a changed lifestyle. God awakens sinners, and God brings them into his family. The result of being a new creation is a transformed lifestyle that pursues good works, unity, and righteousness by relying on God's wisdom and God's Spirit. Conversely, a redeemed sinner puts aside the old way of life and seeks to imitate the love of God.

Unity of the Church

THE WORD *CHURCH* (*EKKLĒSIA*) OCCURS nine times in Ephesians,[1] the highest number of occurrences in all of Paul's letters except 1 Corinthians.[2] The concept of the church as the united body of Christ is also frequently found in Ephesians. Christ is declared the head of the body. As such, he is intimately connected to it but, at the same time, Lord over it. Furthermore, there is only one body, which means that Jew and Gentile alike are united to Christ, and thus to each other, through this body. Christians are therefore urged to walk in unity amid their diversity. Indeed, it is the diverse nature of the church that leads to its maturity.

The Church as the Body of Christ

Among the metaphors that Paul uses for the church, the body of Christ is dominant in Ephesians (and is unique to Paul).[3] The church

---

1 Eph. 1:22; 3:10, 21; 5:23, 24, 25, 27, 29, 32.
2 Second Corinthians also has nine occurrences. Here are the numbers for the rest of Paul's writings: Romans (5), 1 Corinthians (22), Galatians (3), Philippians (2), Colossians (4), 1 Thessalonians (2), 2 Thessalonians (2), 1 Timothy (3), 2 Timothy (0), Titus (0), and Philemon (1).
3 For this and other metaphors, see Daniel L. Akin, ed., *A Theology for the Church*, rev. ed. (Nashville, TN: B&H, 2014), 607–10; Wayne Grudem, *Systematic Theology: An Introduction to Biblical Doctrine*, 2nd ed. (Grand Rapids, MI: Zondervan, 2020), 1052–54; Millard J. Erickson, *Christian Theology* (Grand Rapids, MI: Baker, 1998), 1044–51; Michael F. Bird, *Evangelical Theology: A Biblical and Systematic Introduction*, 2nd ed. (Grand Rapids, MI: Zondervan, 2020), 810–16; Michael Horton, *The Christian Faith: A Systematic Theology for Pilgrims on the Way* (Grand Rapids, MI: Zondervan, 2011), 715–37.

is intimately connected to Christ and is one with him. And yet Paul clarifies that Christ, and Christ alone, as the resurrected and ascended King, is Lord over the church (as well as all other powers or authorities).

In chapter 1 Paul offers a prayer on behalf of the Ephesian believers. At the end of the prayer, he transitions into a statement about the exaltation of Christ. He prays that believers might know the "immeasurable greatness" of God's power toward his people, which is the same power that he worked in Christ (1:19–20). Paul then illustrates the mighty works of God that were accomplished in the Son, specifically his resurrection, his exaltation, the subjugation of his enemies to him, and his dominion.

The first mighty work of God in Christ was the resurrection ("when he raised him from the dead," 1:20). According to the apostles, the resurrection of Jesus is the high point or pinnacle of redemptive history (see Acts 2:23–24; 17:18). Not only did Jesus rise from the dead, but his resurrection signified that he conquered sin and Satan. The resurrection is at the center of God's plan to redeem his people. Second, God's great work in Christ is seen in his exaltation ("seated him at his right hand in the heavenly places," Eph. 1:20). Forty days after the resurrection, Jesus was lifted up and taken into heaven (Acts 1:9) where he is seated on a throne at God's right hand, signifying that his work is finished. Consequently, he now reigns as the sovereign Lord of heaven and earth with power and honor. Third, the enemies of Christ are subjugated to him by God's power ("he put all things under his feet," Eph. 1:22). Although the final subjugation is not yet complete, Paul writes as if it is already accomplished, demonstrating the certainty of God's power and Christ's total rule. Finally, and central to our topic, God's power is displayed in Christ because he is given dominion and headship over the church ("gave him as head over all things to the church," 1:22). Christ has dominion and supremacy over all of creation, including those powers that are hostile to his rule and reign.

Christ's headship, however, extends not only to the hostile forces; it also includes the church. As "head" he is the one who is given the supreme rank and preeminent status over God's people. But not only is Christ head over the church; Paul adjusted the metaphor to proclaim that the church is the body of Christ. Typically, Paul uses the term *church* (*ekklēsia*) to refer to a local gathering of believers.[4] But here, he is referring to the universal church.[5]

The church as the body of Christ occurs several times in Ephesians:

He . . . gave him as head over all things to the *church*, which is his *body*. (1:22–23)

[That he] might reconcile us both to God in *one body* through the cross. (2:16)

There is *one body*. (4:4)

[Christ gives various leaders] to equip the saints for the work of ministry, for building up the *body of Christ*. (4:12)

---

4   See Rom. 16:5; 1 Cor. 1:2; 16:1, 19; 2 Cor. 1:1; 8:1; Gal. 1:2, 22; Col. 4:16; 1 Thess. 1:1; 2:14; 2 Thess. 1:1; Philem. 2.

5   See Eph. 3:10, 21; 5:23–25, 27, 29, 32; Col. 1:18, 24. Often a distinction is made between the universal (invisible) and the local (visible) church. The former refers to all the people of God throughout time, and the latter refers to a specific congregation (or congregations). Because most of the occurrences of *ekklēsia* in the New Testament refer to the local church, Ephesians is said to stand out because of its references to the universal church. Although this description is true, the reason for this distinctive usage is based on the letter's context: (1) Paul refers to Jesus as the head of the church (1:22; 5:23). Jesus is not merely the head over one church or even the churches in a region, but is head over all the churches. (2) Paul's focus on the cosmic and universal rule of Jesus over all powers naturally leads to Christ's rule over the universal church. Jesus is head "over all things" (1:22). It is through the church that God's manifold wisdom is made known "to the rulers and authorities in the heavenly places" (3:10). The glory to God in both the church and in Christ is "throughout all generations" (3:21). (3) The relationship that Christ has with his church (his bride) extends not just to one congregation, but is universal. He loves her (5:25), sacrifices himself for her (5:25), nourishes her (5:29), and ultimately presents her as holy and without blemish (5:27). Consequently, the church submits to Christ (5:25). (4) What is true for the universal church is also true of the local church. After all, Paul is writing to a local church and hopes to influence their thinking and behavior. In other words, we are not speaking about two different entities. Rather, one is a subset (the local church) of the other (the universal church). Furthermore, Paul may be focusing on the heavenly dimension of local churches since the local church is a manifestation of a heavenly reality.

. . . from whom the *whole body*, joined and held together by every joint with which it is equipped, when each part is working properly, makes the body grow so that it builds itself up in love. (4:16)

For the husband is the head of the wife even as Christ is the head of the *church*, his *body*, and is himself its Savior. (5:23)

We are members of his *body*. (5:30)

Paul's Damascus road experience taught him early on the significance of the body of Christ. He learned that he was actually persecuting Jesus when he was persecuting Christians (Acts 9:4; 22:7). Thus the church is organically connected to Christ so that to harm the one is to harm the other. This organic unity is not a fusion of essence but is a communion of persons.[6] Christ is still distinguished from and head over the church. He is the source of the church's life and rules over its affairs. He now works through the church to accomplish his mission. The church, as the one body of Christ, is unified through each member's union with Christ. And because of this unity, there is an interconnectedness or bond between all who are part of the universal church.

Paul engages the metaphor of the church as the body of Christ extensively in Ephesians 5:22–33. Six of the nine occurrences of the term *church* in Ephesians are located in this passage (5:23, 24, 25, 27, 29, 32). Although the broader topic is the relationship between wives and husbands, the relationship between Christ (the husband) and the church (his bride) provides a fitting analogy. Wives are to submit to their husbands as the church submits to Christ, and husbands are to love their wives as Christ loved the church and gave himself up for her.

In 5:23 Paul states, "For the husband is the head of the wife even as Christ is the head of the church, his body, and is himself its Savior." Christ's relation to the church is both as head over it and Savior of it.

6   See Horton, *The Christian Faith*, 736.

Husbands are commanded to love their wives "as Christ loved the church and gave himself up for her" (5:25; see also 5:28, 33; Col. 3:19). The way in which Christ loves his church is the standard by which a husband should love his bride. Specifically, Christ's love is displayed in his self-sacrifice for the church so (1) "that he might sanctify her" (Eph. 5:26) by the cleansing power of the gospel, (2) "that he might present the church to himself in splendor" (5:27), and (3) "that she might be holy and without blemish" (5:27).

Christ has only one body, one bride. The result of this truth is that the church is the single entity that receives his sacrificial love. "There is one body" (4:4). Consequently, the church is unified, even in the midst of the diversity of time, place, and people. In the past, ethnicity was a barrier to joining the people of God but through Christ's sacrifice, the dividing wall of hostility has been destroyed, uniting both Jew and Gentile.

The Church Unified as Jew and Gentile

Peace between Jews and Gentiles (2:14–22)

The destruction of the dividing wall (2:14). Walls do not have to be physical to divide. Metaphorical walls are often more destructive and permanent. In Ephesians, Paul offers a beautiful picture of how Christ's sacrificial death on the cross has torn down the wall that separated Gentiles from God—and thus Gentiles from Jews. In doing so, Christ has created a unified new humanity that is characterized by the term *peace*, a term that occurs four times in this passage (2:14, 15, 17 [2x]).

After urging his Gentile readers to remember their past situation (2:11), Paul calls them to fully embrace their current circumstance—that Christ is their peace. They were "separated from Christ, alienated from the commonwealth of Israel and strangers to the covenants of promise, having no hope and without God in the world" (2:12). But now, through the blood of Christ, they are no longer far off but have been brought near (2:13). The result is not only that we have peace but that Christ *himself* is our peace. That is, he is not only the bringer of peace but also the embodiment of peace. In Colossians, Paul refers to "the peace of

Christ" (Col. 3:15). When Christ is present, peace ensues, and this peace brings certain consequences. First, he has made both Jewish and Gentile believers one (Eph. 2:14). The former hostility and discord between these two ethnic groups has been eliminated and replaced with peace.

The second consequence of Christ's peace-securing work on the cross is that he has "broken down in his flesh the dividing wall of hostility" (2:14). Metaphorically, the wall could refer to the Mosaic Law, which set the Jews apart from the Gentiles. More specifically, the food laws, Sabbath restrictions, and circumcision would have separated the Jewish people from the pagan religions around them. This cultural and religious separation also had a physical representation as the Jews erected a "dividing wall" around the temple, which separated the inner courts from the Court of the Gentiles. That is, Gentiles were allowed into the temple compound but were restricted from entering the grounds directly surrounding the temple itself. The first-century Jewish historian Josephus describes a wall, four and a half feet tall, with warning signs posted in various places around the wall in both Greek and Latin. Two of these signs have been discovered and state: "No foreigner is to enter within the railing and enclosure around the Temple. Whoever is caught shall have himself to blame for his consequent death."[7] Because Paul uses a different term in Ephesians (*phragmos*) than the one found on the warning mentioned by Josephus (*truphraktos*) and because there is uncertainty whether Paul's Gentile readers in Ephesus would have been familiar with the inner wall around the temple, this connection should not be unduly pressed. Even if Paul was alluding to this physical dividing, it was merely a physical representation of a deeper reality: certain people were excluded from the presence of God if they did not meet certain qualifications. In the gospel, however, this wall has been taken down and Jesus has become the perfect priest who is able to enter the presence of God on our behalf. The wall has been removed. Access to God is available through the perfect mediator between God and men, the man Christ Jesus (1 Tim. 2:5).

7   See Josephus, *Ant.* 15.11.5; *J.W.* 5.5.2 (author's translation).

The abolishing of the law (2:15–17). By means of his death on the cross ("in his flesh"), Christ has demolished the dividing wall and abolished the law of commandments (cf. Col. 1:22; 2:14). What does it mean that the law has been abolished? Based on what Paul says elsewhere, it does not mean that the law is completely useless or destroyed. In Romans 3:31 Paul writes, "Do we then overthrow the law by this faith? By no means! On the contrary, we uphold the law." The law is not cancelled or nullified by the gospel. Rather, the Mosaic Law, which was associated with the Mosaic covenant, is set aside because that covenant was fulfilled in Christ. As Thielman rightly notes:

> The Mosaic law was still authoritative Scripture with the new people of God, but in a different way than it had been for Israel. It revealed the character of God, the nature of humanity, and the centrality of faith to a right relationship with God, but its commandments no longer governed the behavior of God's people without first passing through the filter of the gospel.[8]

Although some have qualified Paul's meaning by claiming that it applies only to the ceremonial and civil aspects of the Mosaic Law (and not to the moral laws), such a division is somewhat artificial. It is best to interpret Paul's reference to the law as referring to the law in its entirety. "For when there is a change in the priesthood, there is necessarily a change in the law as well" (Heb. 7:12). With the coming of Christ, the new high priest, the old law is set aside and the law of Christ is ratified (Gal. 6:2).

When Christ destroyed the dividing wall and abolished the law, the result was that he created "one new man" (Eph. 2:15). He united both Jew and Gentile believers, creating a new humanity, a new creation.

---

8   Frank Thielman, *Ephesians*, BECNT (Grand Rapids, MI: Baker, 2010), 170. See also Jason C. Meyer, "The Mosaic Law, Theological Systems, and the Glory of Christ," in *Progressive Covenantalism: Charting a Course between Dispensational and Covenant Theologies*, ed. Stephen J. Wellum and Brent E. Parker (Nashville, TN: B&H Academic, 2016), 69–99.

Earlier Paul states that believers are God's "workmanship" who are "created" in Christ for good works (2:10). That is, through his death, Christ has brought together both Jew and Gentile to form a new humanity. Elsewhere Paul states, "Therefore, if anyone is in Christ, he is a new creation. The old has passed away; behold, the new has come" (2 Cor. 5:17), and "For neither circumcision counts for anything, nor uncircumcision, but a new creation" (Gal. 6:15). The resulting status between Jewish and Gentile believers is peace. The enmity of the law is now removed, and God's peace is established.

The reason why Jew and Gentile can be reconciled to each other is that they can first be reconciled "to God in one body through the cross" (Eph. 2:16). In other words, horizontal peace and reconciliation are now possible because vertical peace and reconciliation between God and humanity are now possible through the redeeming work of Christ. Believing Jews and Gentiles are united into a new humanity because they are first united to God. In Colossians Paul writes that Christ came "to reconcile to himself all things, whether on earth or in heaven, making peace by the blood of his cross. And you, who once were alienated and hostile in mind, doing evil deeds, he has now reconciled in his body of flesh by his death, in order to present you holy and blameless and above reproach before him" (Col. 1:20–22). Christ abolished the law for the purpose of reconciling both Jews and Gentiles to God "in one body," which is not a reference to the crucified body of Christ but to the "one new man" (Eph. 2:15), the church. Paul thoroughly grounds the reconciliation and resulting peace in the ministry and work of Christ. It was accomplished "by the blood of Christ" (2:13), "in his flesh" (2:14), and "through the cross" (2:16). The anger and wrath of God (Rom. 1:18) have been appeased through the atoning and reconciling work of Christ.

The bringing of peace (2:17–18). Earlier Paul states that Christ is our "peace" (Eph. 2:14) and has made "peace" (2:15). In this passage Paul notes that Christ "came and preached peace to you who were far off and peace to those who were near" (2:17). That is, in his earthly ministry and/or through his apostles, Jesus preached peace to Gentiles and to Jews. Later Paul explains that the gospel ("the mystery of Christ," 3:4) "has now been revealed to his holy apostles and prophets by the Spirit" (3:5) and that he received grace "to preach to the Gentiles the unsearchable riches of Christ" (3:8).

The message of the gospel is thus a proclamation of peace—peace between a holy God and sinful humanity. Although the peace here primarily refers to the reconciliation between God and humanity, it clearly has implications for the relationship between Gentiles (those "far off") and Jews (those "near"). Paul's language is likely drawn from Isaiah: "How beautiful upon the mountains are the feet of him who brings good news, who publishes peace" (Isa. 52:7), and "'Peace, peace, to the far and to the near,' says the LORD" (Isa. 57:19). The reason that peace can be proclaimed to Jews and Gentiles is that "access" to God is secured through Christ: "For through him we both have access in one Spirit to the Father" (Eph. 2:18). Whereas in the Old Testament access to God was severely restricted, believers can now enter into the presence of God through Christ's atoning and reconciling work. In Christ, "we have boldness and access with confidence through our faith in him" (3:12). "Therefore, since we have been justified by faith, we have peace with God through our Lord Jesus Christ. Through him we have also obtained access by faith into this grace in which we stand, and we rejoice in hope of the glory of God" (Rom. 5:1–2). The Trinitarian emphasis is hard to miss: believers have peace and access through Christ, in the Spirit, to the Father.

The reality of a new status (2:19–22). The result of peace and reconciliation is the new status of God's people as (1) citizens in God's kingdom, (2) members of God's household, and (3) integral parts of God's temple. First, Paul uses a political metaphor to convey the new status of believers. No longer are Gentiles *strangers* to the covenants of promise (Eph. 2:12), but they are now "fellow citizens" (2:19). Believers who were once considered foreigners are now citizens in God's kingdom. Elsewhere Paul reminds us that "our citizenship is in heaven" (Phil. 3:20). All believers are fellow citizens and have a common homeland as citizens of God's heavenly kingdom.

Second, Paul uses a familial metaphor to explicate the results of Christ's reconciling work. He states that Gentiles are no longer "aliens" but are now "members of the household of God" (Eph. 2:19). An "alien" is someone who lives as a foreigner in a land, not having certain rights and privileges. But now, through Christ, those who were once estranged from God have been welcomed into God's household. That is, they have been adopted and granted all the rights and privileges of a full-fledged member of the family (see also Gal. 6:10; 1 Tim. 5:8). Paul has already highlighted the blessing of being *adopted* in Christ (Eph. 1:5) and has just written about the access we have *to the Father* through Christ (2:18). Here, Paul uses the household language to give assurance and confidence to his Gentile readers that their heavenly Father receives them as his children and will protect them and provide for them.

Third, Paul uses a cultic metaphor to convey the reality of the new status of believers. Because of the reconciling work of Christ, believers are now building stones in God's holy temple. The temple is the house or dwelling place of God. Paul offers at least six characteristics of this spiritual temple. First, this temple is built by God himself (2:20, 22). Paul twice uses the divine passive to signify that God is the one who is building this temple: it is "built" (2:20) on a secure foundation and together believers "are being built" (2:22) as a dwelling place for God. Second, the temple is "built on the foundation of the apostles and prophets" (2:20). The New Testament apostles and prophets (and their ministry) form the foundation of the church. The "apostles" are those who were chosen, commissioned, and sent by Jesus. They included the twelve, Paul, and possibly a few others (Acts 1:21–22; 1 Cor. 15:7; Gal. 1:19; 2:7–9). The "prophets" were spirit-endowed individuals who communicated the revelation of God to edify, comfort, and encourage the church. Thus believers are built upon the authoritative and normative teaching of the apostles and prophets that arose from divine revelation. Third, Jesus is the "cornerstone" of the temple (Eph. 2:20; see also 1 Pet. 2:6), likely an allusion to Isaiah 28:16 (the only place in the Old Testament where the term is found): "Therefore thus says the Lord God, 'Behold, I am the one who has laid as a foundation in Zion, a stone, a tested stone, a precious cornerstone, of a sure foundation: "Whoever believes will not be in haste."'''' The cornerstone is the most important stone of the foundation, bearing the weight of the building and tying the walls firmly together. Christ is the ultimate foundation (1 Cor. 3:11) since he is the vital cornerstone.

Fourth, only through union with Christ does one join this spiritual temple (Eph. 2:21–22). Fifth, this temple is not complete but is growing (2:21; see also 4:16). The growth is both spiritual (into a *holy* temple) and numerical (Gentiles are added). Sixth, the temple is a dwelling place of God (2:22). In the Old Testament, God's presence was uniquely located in the temple. In 1 Corinthians, Paul writes, "Do you not know that you are God's temple and that God's Spirit dwells in you? If anyone destroys God's temple, God will destroy him. For God's temple is holy, and you are that temple" (1 Cor. 3:16–17). Later he writes (quoting Lev. 26:12), "We are the temple of the living God; as God said, 'I will make my dwelling among them and walk among them, and I will be their God, and they shall be my people'" (2 Cor. 6:16). Thus God is building this temple as a dwelling place for himself by his Spirit.

The status of Gentiles who now believe in Jesus as the Messiah has been completely reversed. Those who were Christ-less ("separated from Christ"), homeless ("alienated from the commonwealth of Israel"), friendless ("strangers to the covenants of promise"), hopeless ("having no hope"), and godless ("without God") now are citizens, members, and God's dwelling place. Jesus is the "Prince of Peace" (Isa. 9:6) who has brought peace to his people (John 14:27; Eph. 2:17). The church, composed of both Jew and Gentile believers, is built on the same foundation (apostles and prophets) and has the same cornerstone (Jesus Christ). Christ has unified his people by destroying the dividing wall, abolishing the law, bringing peace, and granting a new status to his people.

Unity in the Church (4:1–6)

The focus of 4:1–6 is the unity of the church. Paul urges believers to walk in a manner worthy of their calling (4:1), a manner primarily consisting of certain attitudes (humility, gentleness, patience, and love, 4:2) that promote a unified spirit among believers ("the unity of the Spirit in the bond of peace," 4:3). The second part of this passage (4:4–6) emphasizes the basis of believers' unity, which is grounded in the unity of God (one Spirit . . . one Lord . . . one God and Father of all), the unity of the people of God (one body), and the unity of the church's response to God (one hope . . . one faith, one baptism).

The Way of Unity (4:1–3)

Ephesians 4 marks a transition from the doctrinal section to the practical section of the letter. Paul exhorts his readers to walk or live worthy of their calling, which, in the context, is an exhortation specifically to unity:

> I . . . urge you to walk in a manner worthy of the calling to which you have been called, with all humility and gentleness, with patience, bearing with one another in love, eager to maintain the unity of the Spirit in the bond of peace. (4:1–3)

Verses 2 and 3 provide the way in which unity can be attained. It involves an attitude or disposition of humility, gentleness, and patience and the actions or deeds of bearing with others and eagerly keeping the unity of the Spirit.

Paul lists three virtues that describe the attitudes in which we are to walk: "with all humility and gentleness, with patience" (4:2). With Paul's emphasis on unity and oneness in this section, it is easy to see why humility is stressed. "Few things are more destructive to community life than pride and arrogance."[9] Indeed, "God opposes the proud but gives grace to the humble" (1 Pet. 5:5). Jesus himself is our model of humility (Phil. 2:1–11). Paul lists gentleness as one of the fruits of the Spirit in Galatians 5:23, and he emphasizes it as that which is needed when restoring someone who has sinned (Gal. 6:1) and for correcting someone who is in error (2 Tim. 2:25). The third virtue that is needed

---

9   Clinton E. Arnold, *Ephesians*, ZECNT (Grand Rapids, MI: Zondervan, 2010), 229.

for unity is "patience," a characteristic mentioned repeatedly in the Bible regarding God (see Ex. 34:6). God's kindness and patience are what lead us to repentance (Rom. 2:4) since he does not want anyone to perish (2 Pet. 3:9). Patience is a fruit of the Spirit (Gal. 5:22), a defining quality of love (1 Cor. 13:4), and a characteristic that Christians are to display toward one another (Col. 3:12; 1 Thess. 5:14; 2 Tim. 4:2).

Unity requires not only the embrace of certain attitudes, but it also requires certain actions. First, unity is achieved by "bearing with one another in love" (Eph. 4:2). *Bearing*, a verb often used in contexts of enduring suffering or persecution (1 Cor. 4:12; 2 Cor. 11:20; 2 Thess. 1:4), conveys that such actions can be difficult. But Paul is not simply suggesting that believers *tolerate* each other but that we bear with each other "in love." In Colossians 3:13 Paul adds, "if one has a complaint against another, forgiving each other." Second, for unity to be attained, believers must be "eager to maintain the unity of the Spirit" (Eph. 4:3). The term *eager* adds urgency to this appeal, used elsewhere by Paul to communicate the intense effort and labor involved in making a trip or journey (1 Thess. 2:17; 2 Tim. 4:9, 21; Titus 3:12). Furthermore, it is used by Peter to urge his readers to "be all the more diligent to confirm your calling and election" (2 Pet. 1:10) and "be diligent to be found by him without spot or blemish" (2 Pet. 3:14). Paul is not exhorting his readers to *create* unity but rather to *maintain* the unity that already exists based on the finished work of Christ (Eph. 2:11–22). This unity comes from the Holy Spirit. Consequently, believers are exhorted to maintain the unity that has been secured by Christ and is given by the Spirit.

Unity is not optional for believers, but it is part and parcel of the very message we proclaim. When we believers fail to live in unity and peace with one another, our message is compromised. Jesus prayed, "The glory that you have given me I have given to them, that they may be one even as we are one, I in them and you in me, that they may become perfectly one, so that the world may know that you sent me and loved them even as you loved me" (John 17:22–23). Thus the unity of believers impacts their testimony to the world. Unity is not an option for Christians but is at the very heart of our faith.

If unity is to be achieved in the church, it requires humility, gentleness, patience, tolerance, love, and peace. Humility is needed because pride insists on getting its way. Gentleness is needed because anger offends and harms others. Patience is needed because we cannot control the actions of others, especially God's actions. Tolerance is needed because everybody has weaknesses. Love is needed because it is the oil that lubricates all the other virtues. And peace is needed because unity cannot truly exist without God's people being united by the peace that passes all understanding (Phil. 4:7).

The Why of Unity (4:4–6)

After summoning his readers to walk in the way of unity, Paul then shifts to the why of unity. That is, in this passage he provides the grounds or theological basis for the unity that is possible among believers:

> There is one body and one Spirit—just as you were called to the one hope that belongs to your call—one Lord, one faith, one baptism, one God and Father of all, who is over all and through all and in all. (Eph. 4:4–6)

In these three short verses Paul emphasizes the unity of the church by the sevenfold repetition of "one." First, Paul indicates that the church, the body of Christ, is "one body" (4:4; see also 1:22–23).[10] Because unity of the church is the apostle's primary concern, he highlights it by placing it first in his list. Even though the church is composed of many members with different gifts, together they form one body that is united through their relationship with Christ. Second, Paul indicates that there is "one Spirit" (4:4), a phrase that is also found in 1 Corinthians 12:11 (those gifted are empowered by "one and the same Spirit") and 12:13 (in "one Spirit" believers were baptized into one body). Paul has already mentioned that believers (1) are sealed

---

10 For other references to the church as "one body," see Rom. 12:4–5; 1 Cor. 12:12–13, 20; Col. 3:15.

with the Spirit (Eph. 1:13), (2) have access to the Father through the Spirit (2:18), (3) are a dwelling place for God by the Spirit (2:22), and (4) are strengthened in the inner man through the Spirit (3:16). Third, believers are called to "one hope" (4:4). Just as there is one body and one Spirit, there is also one hope that accompanied their call. The hope to which Paul is referring is not the subjective feeling of a confident expectation but its objective content.

Fourth, the apostle adds that there is "one Lord" (4:5), a clear reference to Jesus Christ. Against the claims of Caesar or others who may have claimed such a title, Paul affirms that there is only one who can rightfully claim that appellation (see Rom. 10:9; 1 Cor. 12:3; Phil. 2:11). Furthermore, this declaration identifies Jesus with the God of the Old Testament (Deut. 6:4). Fifth, Paul acknowledges "one faith" (Eph. 4:5), a reference to the objective content of what is believed (and not the subjective act of believing).[11] Sixth, there is "one baptism" (4:5), a reference to water baptism and the accompanying Spirit baptism associated with it. As Bruce explains, "It is Christian baptism—baptism 'into the name of the Lord Jesus' (Acts 8:16; 19:5; cf. 1 Cor. 1:13–15)—which indeed involved the application of water . . . but . . . was closely associated with the gift of the Spirit."[12]

Seventh, Paul ends his sevenfold emphasis on the unity of the church by adding that there is "one God and Father of all" (Eph. 4:6). The oneness of God is a fundamental belief in Scripture (Deut. 6:4), and the fatherhood of God is prominent in the New Testament.[13] This verse affirms God's "supreme transcendence" (he is "over all") as well as his "pervasive immanence" (he is "through all and in all").[14] Paul declares God's supreme sovereignty, omnipotence, and presence in his creation. Finally, the divine Trinity is central to Paul's discussion

---

11 For references to the objective faith of what is believed, see 4:13; Rom. 10:8; Gal. 1:23; 3:23; Col. 1:23; 2:7; 1 Tim. 3:9; 4:1, 6.

12 F. F. Bruce, *Colossians, Philemon, Ephesians*, NICNT (Grand Rapids, MI: Eerdmans, 1984), 336–37.

13 For the phrase "God and Father," see Rom. 15:6; 2 Cor. 1:3; 11:31; Gal. 1:4; Eph. 1:3; Phil. 4:20; 1 Thess. 3:11, 13; 1 Pet. 1:3; Rev. 1:6.

14 Andrew D. Lincoln, *Ephesians*, WBC 42 (Dallas: Word, 1990), 240.

on unity. The *Spirit* is linked with the one body or church, which is called in one hope. The *Lord* is linked with the one faith the church professes and the one baptism it receives. Finally, *God the Father* is the one who supremely rules over all his creation and yet is intimately involved working in and through all things. Only a unity that is theologically grounded in the reality of the triune God and his gospel will be able to survive the attacks from without and the pressure from within.

The Church Diversified for Maturity (4:7–16)

A Diversity of Gifted Individuals (4:7–10)

Although the church possesses a fundamental unity, it is also diversified for the purpose of building up the body of believers. That is, Christ has variously gifted his church so that the community of believers would be edified. In Ephesians 4:7 Paul states that "grace was given to each one of us according to the measure of Christ's gift." This verse highlights Christ's role in sovereignly gifting individual believers to build up the church. The "grace" that is given refers to ministry grace, not to saving or sanctifying grace. This grace is specifically given to every believer ("to each one of us") by the risen and ascended Savior. Furthermore, these gifts are not based on works or merit but are "according to the measure of Christ's gift." Christ graciously and sovereignly distributes gifts to every member of his body.

The citation of Psalm 68:18 in 4:8 provides support for the claim that Christ has gifted each member of his body. Paul's citation, however, does not exactly follow the Hebrew Old Testament or the Greek Septuagint.

> You ascended to the high places, you captured captives, you received gifts from mankind. (Ps. 67:19 LXX)

> When he ascended to the high places, he captured captives, he gave gifts to men. (Eph. 4:8)[15]

---

15 Translations of both the Septuagint (LXX) and the Greek New Testament are the author's.

Even though there are noticeable differences (change from second to third person, change of the verb "received" to "gave," and the change of the preposition "from mankind" to "to men"), Paul stays true to the intent of the passage, offering a Christological interpretation.[16] In the psalm, God is the divine warrior who ascends to his throne after defeating his enemies. In Ephesians, Christ is the victorious conqueror who ascends to his throne in heaven after defeating the spiritual forces. But instead of receiving gifts (i.e., the spoils of war) from those vanquished, the resurrected and ascended Christ sovereignly gives gifts to his followers. Thielman accurately observes, "Although Paul has changed the wording of verse 18 . . . he has done so in a way that is consistent with the psalm's theme of God's triumph over the enemies of his people."[17] The following verses, 4:9–10, provide an inspired commentary on Psalm 68:18, specifically the descent and ascent of Christ "far above all the heavens" (Eph. 4:10). Christ's status is as the risen Messiah seated at the Father's right hand. Christ has thus ascended to the place of highest supremacy.

A Diversity That Leads to Maturity (4:11–16)

The conquering, resurrected, and ascended Christ graciously gifts each believer in his church so that the church will become mature. The gifts given by Christ are not merely spiritual gifts but are the persons themselves given for the unity and maturity of the church: "And

---

16 Paul's interpretation and use of Psalm 68 is similar to the Aramaic Targum ("you gave gifts to the sons of men") and the Syriac Peshitta, though he adds a Christological element (see Arnold, *Ephesians*, 251–52; Markus Barth, *Ephesians 4–6*, AB 34 [Garden City, NY: Doubleday, 1974], 2:476; Lincoln, *Ephesians*, 243–44; William J. Larkin, *Ephesians: A Handbook on the Greek Text*, BHGNT [Waco, TX: Baylor University Press, 2009], 75). Others believe that Paul's changes are not based on the Targum but still represent the essence of the original context (Thielman, *Ephesians*, 267–68; Harold W. Hoehner, *Ephesians: An Exegetical Commentary* [Grand Rapids, MI: Baker, 2002], 528). Still others maintain that the military language of Psalm 68 is poetic and the captive prisoners are not defeated Gentile enemies but are rebellious Israelites (see Num. 8, 18). Thus Paul's exegesis is "but a remoulding of the thought of Psalm 68:18 on the basis of Scriptural commentary in Numbers 8:6–19; 18:6 which the Psalmist used" (G. V. Smith, "Paul's Use of Psalm 68:18 in Ephesians 4:8," *JETS* [1985]: 189).

17 Thielman, *Ephesians*, 268.

he gave the apostles, the prophets, the evangelists, the shepherds and teachers" (4:11). Paul includes five types of individuals who are gifted by Christ and given to the church. First, he has given apostles to the church. Paul labels himself an apostle (1:1) but also states that apostles (along with prophets) provide the foundation for the church (2:20). Prophets are not Old Testament prophets but are those alive during Paul's time who spoke God's truth to the church. Earlier, Paul explains that the mystery that the Jews and Gentiles would be joined together into the body of Christ "was not made known to the sons of men in other generations as it has now been revealed to his holy apostles and prophets by the Spirit" (3:5). The term *evangelist* is used only two other times in the New Testament (Acts 21:8; 2 Tim. 4:5), and evangelists "are probably those whom God has especially equipped to travel from place to place with the good news of peace through Christ."[18] This description would apply to both Philip (who traveled around preaching the gospel; Acts 8:4–5, 35, 40) and Timothy (who was only temporarily in Ephesus and would soon be traveling again; 2 Tim. 4:9, 21). The final two terms, "shepherds" (or "pastors") and "teachers" are best seen not as two distinct groups but as overlapping. In other words, "pastors" is a subset of "teachers" because all pastors teach, but not all teachers are also pastors.[19] Despite its common use in many churches today, this is the only place in the New Testament that the term *pastor* is applied to someone who holds a ministry position in the church (though the verbal form is sometimes used; see Acts 20:28; 1 Pet. 5:2).

In Ephesians 4:12 Paul offers the reason why Christ has given leaders to the church: "to equip the saints for the work of ministry, for building up the body of Christ." The diversity of gifted individuals is what leads to maturity in the body. Unfortunately, there is a lack of clarity as to Paul's meaning here. Because the KJV places a comma after every prepositional phrase, they are each viewed as coordinate or parallel. If that is the case, then Christ gave various ministers to the church in

18   Thielman, *Ephesians*, 274.

19   See Daniel B. Wallace, *Greek Grammar beyond the Basics* (Grand Rapids, MI: Zondervan, 1996), 284.

order to accomplish three things: (1) the perfecting of the saints, (2) the work of the ministry, (3) the edifying of the body of Christ. In this reading of the text, it is the leaders who do the work of the ministry and not the equipped saints. It is better, however, to interpret the second phrase as dependent on the first and the third phrase as dependent on the first two. Consequently, Christ gives leaders who equip the saints, and it is the *saints* who do the work of the ministry (and not merely the leaders). This interpretation is supported by the Greek that uses two different prepositions to mark this distinction as well as the context with its emphasis on gifts given "to each one" (4:7) so that "each part" (4:16) does its work.[20]

If this reading of the text is correct, it greatly impacts how we view church leadership and the nature of ministry in the church. The task of church leaders is "to equip the saints for the work of ministry" (4:12). Their goal is not simply to do the work of ministry but rather to equip all believers to somehow participate in ministry. In other words, "ministry" is not limited to those who are the designated leaders of the church. Rather, Christ gifts leaders whose task it is to equip all the saints to do the work of the ministry. A formal clergy-laity distinction is not found in Paul. This passage affirms the priesthood of all believers, which claims that there is no special status of priest among Christians but that *all* are called as priests to serve God. All believers should be equipped "for building up the body of Christ" (4:12). The goal for Christ gifting the church with leaders is so that his body, the church, will become spiritually mature.

And yet we must not deny that Christ has gifted certain individuals to be leaders in his church. Not all have the same gifts or the same measure of giftedness. Some are called to be apostles, prophets, evangelists, or pastor-teachers. Interestingly, all of these leaders primarily possess gifts of speech—that is, a ministry of speaking or teaching God's word that is vital for the unity and maturity of God's people.

---

20 The ESV accurately reflects this distinction in English: "to [*pros*] equip the saints for [*eis*] the work of ministry, for [*eis*] building up the body of Christ."

Teaching gifts and abilities are also emphasized in the qualifications for overseers/elders (1 Tim. 3:2; Titus 1:9). Christ gifts all, but some are given the special responsibility of equipping the saints to properly understand God's word so that they will be equipped to do the work of the ministry.

In Ephesians 4:13 Paul affirms that the church must be built up "until we all attain" three particular goals: (1) "the unity of the faith and of the knowledge of the Son of God," (2) "mature manhood," and (3) "the measure of the stature of the fullness of Christ."[21] By "unity of the faith," Paul is declaring that believers should be in agreement concerning the apostolic teaching found in the Bible (see Jude 3). Similarly, the "knowledge" of God's Son refers to those truths about Jesus that are essential for all believers to affirm. Biblical unity must be founded on the objective truth-claims of Jesus. Paul adds that God's people should together attain to "mature manhood." Interestingly, Paul uses the term *manhood* (*anēr*), which is gender and age specific. Thielman maintains that the reason for this usage "may be the result of Paul's desire to contrast human maturity with immaturity, since in the next verse he will say that once all believers have arrived at the goal of maturity, they will no longer be 'infants.'"[22] Finally, God's desire is for his people to attain the maturity that Christ himself possesses ("the measure of the stature of the fullness of Christ"). In other words, "the glorified Christ provides the standard at which his people are to aim: the corporate Christ [i.e., the church] cannot be content to fall short of the perfection of the person Christ."[23] If only a few gifted leaders do the work of the ministry, churches might grow in numbers but not in depth of maturity. The primary goal of the ministry is to build up the body of Christ so that every member attains Christlikeness. When the leaders actively equip the other members to serve, such a goal is within reach.

Paul contrasts the mature man (Eph. 4:13) with immature children (4:14). The goal is "that we may no longer be children," which

---

21 Each of these purpose statements is introduced by the preposition *eis*.

22 Thielman, *Ephesians*, 282.

23 Bruce, *Colossians, Philemon, Ephesians*, 350–51.

"has reference to a child's gullibility, lack of understanding or lack of perception."[24] This metaphorical use of *children* refers to spiritually immature believers. Paul then shifts metaphors from human development to seafaring imagery. Those who are immature are "tossed to and fro by the waves and carried about" (4:14). This imagery further emphasizes lack of maturity since such people have little ability to defend themselves against the wind and the waves. First, these immature believers are tossed and blown "by every wind of doctrine" (4:14). Lincoln suggests that this phrase is "a reference to false teaching in the guise of the various religious philosophies which threatened to assimilate, and thereby dilute or undermine, the Pauline gospel."[25] Second, they are tossed and blown "by human cunning" (4:14). Arnold notes that "cunning" (sometimes translated "trickery") "is a rare word that never appears in the LXX or Jewish literature. In Greek literature it commonly refers to dice playing and, consequently, the forms of trickery that often accompanied gambling."[26] Third, they are tossed and blown "by craftiness in deceitful schemes" (4:14). Believers are therefore encouraged to be firmly grounded in the apostolic teaching so that they may develop and grow into mature followers of Christ.

For the church to become mature, it requires that we speak "the truth in love" (4:15), which refers to more than just honest speech but relates to speaking or confessing the truth of the gospel lovingly. Again, the desired goal is maturity: "to grow up in every way into him" (4:15; see also Heb. 5:12–6:1). Christians are not to remain as children in their faith but are to become more like their Savior. Christ, as the head of the church, is the one who leads the church and the one who nourishes and supplies all that the body needs for its growth. All believers ("every joint," Eph. 4:16) are gifted, joined together, and empowered by God to use their gifts for the benefit of others and for the common good. The end result is that the body grows in maturity.

24 Hoehner, *Ephesians*, 560–61.
25 Lincoln, *Ephesians*, 258.
26 Arnold, *Ephesians*, 268.

Summary

The church is the means through which God establishes and spreads his kingdom on earth. With the resurrected and ascended Christ as the head of the church, "the gates of hell shall not prevail against it" (Matt. 16:18). The reconciliation that Christ established through his work on the cross results in peace between God and humanity *and* peace between Jews and Gentiles. The dividing wall of hostility has been torn down resulting in the creation of a new, unified humanity. But unity in the church, though it is objective reality, is subjectively something that needs to be pursued with humility, gentleness, patience, and love. Finally, the unity of the church does not mean uniformity since Christ has gifted each individual uniquely. Leaders are given to the church so that all members will become mature and Christlike in how they think and how they live.

Spiritual Warfare in the Present Age

THE BOOK OF EPHESIANS HAS THE longest discussion about spiritual warfare in the New Testament (6:10–20). But Paul's specific instruction regarding believers' spiritual battle is not merely an appendix at the end of an epistle. Rather, it is the culmination of teaching and prayers that have been presented throughout the letter. In fact, Ephesus was known for its magic practices. In Acts 19 we read, "Also many of those who were now believers came, confessing and divulging their practices. And a number of those who had practiced magic arts brought their books together and burned them in the sight of all. And they counted the value of them and found it came to fifty thousand pieces of silver" (Acts 19:18–19). Although magic practices were prevalent in the Hellenistic world, they were especially widespread in Ephesus, which housed the temple of Artemis. Clinton Arnold, in his book *Power and Magic: The Concept of Power in Ephesians*, explains why Paul uses a high concentration of "power" language in this epistle:

> Ephesians appears to have been written to a group of churches in western Asia Minor needing help in developing a Christian perspective on the "powers" and encouragement in their ongoing struggles with these pernicious spirit-forces. . . . The teaching of the epistle on power, while universally relevant and applicable, would prove

particularly helpful to converts from a background of strong demonic beliefs and fears.[1]

Therefore, Paul seeks to assuage these fears by reminding his readers about the supremacy of Jesus. Even divine election and union with Christ may be emphasized by Paul for this reason. Before their conversion, they were controlled by beliefs in false gods who supposedly held sway over the direction of their lives. But now they receive comfort and security knowing that God had chosen them before the world was created (Eph. 1:5). Their fear of cosmic forces who once weakened them into submission has been supplanted by the assurance that they are now identified with and united to Christ. He is the risen Lord who has defeated all enemies, triumphing over them on the cross and further establishing his dominion through his exaltation. Because believers are now identified with Christ, they are victorious over all hostile powers even if the current situation requires that they battle against these defeated foes. As Arnold writes:

> Their perceived weakness and vulnerability before the cosmic "powers" needs to be supplanted by the confidence which comes from knowing that they are intimately identified with their risen and victorious Lord. His victory over the "powers" is their victory. His present authority over the "powers" is their authority.[2]

In this section, we will first consider the present rule of Satan. He is presently ruling and influencing the lives of unbelievers and sometimes even believers. Second, we will discuss the present reign of Christ. Although Satan has some rule over this world, Jesus is the King who reigns over all creation. Third, we will detail how Christians are cur-

---

1   Clinton E. Arnold, *Power and Magic: The Concept of Power in Ephesians* (Eugene, OR: Wipf & Stock, 1989), 167, 168. "Power" terminology includes: "power" (*dunamis*: 1:19, 21; 3:7, 16, 20), "working" (*energeia*: 3:7; 4:16), "strength" (*ischuos*: 1:19; 6:10), "might" (*kratos*: 1:19; 6:10), "authority" (*exousia*: 1:21; 2:2; 3:10; 6:12), "to be able/powerful" (*dunamai*: 3:4, 20; 6:11, 13, 16), "to strengthen" (*endunamoō*: 6:10), "to strengthen" (*krataioō*: 3:16), and "to be able/strong" (*exischuō*: 3:18).

2   Arnold, *Power and Magic*, 137.

rently engaged in a spiritual battle and how we must wrestle and fight against an unseen foe. Finally, we will analyze Paul's teaching on the present age and the age to come.

The Present Rule of Satan

In Ephesians, Satan is called the "devil" (4:27; 6:11), the "evil one" (6:16), the "prince [or "ruler," *archōn*] of the power of the air" (2:2), and the "spirit [*pneuma*] that is now at work in the sons of disobedience" (2:2). In the Old Testament, Satan (i.e., "the accuser") is a supernatural being who was originally created by God as good. But now he is an evil being who opposes God and his people. He is the leader of cosmic forces who rebel against God. He is subject to God, and therefore his powers are limited. The designation "Satan" (*satana*) is found thirty-six times in the New Testament and ten times in Paul, though it never occurs in Ephesians.[3] Instead, Paul uses "devil" twice (4:27; 6:11), a term that is only found in Ephesians and the Pastoral Epistles in the New Testament.[4] "Devil" is not a personal name but rather a term that means "slanderer" or "adversary."

Satan's Kingdom

In 2 Corinthians, Paul calls Satan "the god of this world" (4:4). Thus "Paul clearly distinguishes between two kingdoms in the present age: the kingdom of Christ and the kingdom of Satan."[5] Specifically, Satan "has blinded the minds of the unbelievers" so that they do not see "the light of the gospel of the glory of Christ" (2 Cor. 4:4). The gospel message of a crucified but risen and exalted Messiah "heralds the dawn of a new age and the passing of the old along with its dark lord."[6] Thus "Satan is vested with a sovereignty, however limited it might ultimately be, that is powerful, compelling and clearly opposed to the work of God in Christ."[7]

---

3   The Pauline occurrences of "Satan" are Rom. 16:20; 1 Cor. 5:5; 7:5; 2 Cor. 2:11; 11:14; 12:7; 1 Thess. 2:18; 2 Thess. 2:9; 1 Tim. 1:20; 5:15.

4   The occurrences of "devil" in the Pastoral Epistles are 1 Tim. 3:6, 7; 2 Tim. 2:26; 3:3; Titus 2:3.

5   D. G. Reid, "Satan, Devil," in *DPL* 864.

6   Reid, "Satan," 864.

7   Reid, "Satan," 864.

Ephesians (and Colossians) also presents a view of reality that includes two kingdoms. Those who have placed their faith in Christ have been delivered "from the domain of darkness and transferred . . . to the kingdom of his beloved Son" (Col. 1:13). Here, Paul contrasts the "domain" (*exousia*) of Satan with the "kingdom" (*basileia*) of Christ. In Ephesians, Satan is characterized as the "prince of the power [*exousia*] of the air" (2:2). "Power" indicates the sphere or domain in which his authority is exercised. Satan's realm of influence or authority is specifically as the prince or ruler of the "air" (*aēr*), which may be related to the "heavenly places" that are inhabited by evil principalities and powers (3:10; 6:12).

In the Gospel of John, three times Satan is called the "ruler [*archōn*] of this world" (John 12:31; 14:30; 16:11). Interestingly, each time, Jesus offers some limitation or negative aspect to the ruling power of Satan. In John 12:31 Jesus states, "Now is the judgment of this world; now will the ruler of this world be cast out." Although Satan is named the "ruler of this world," he is also the recipient of God's judgment because of the victory of Jesus secured by his cross work. In other words, it is on the cross that the decisive battle is won. It is through the cross that Jesus dethrones (casts out) Satan and takes his place as the rightful King. In John 14:30 Jesus clarifies that even though he is returning to the Father and that Satan, the ruler of this world, is coming, Satan "has no claim on me." Jesus's point here is "to declare this cosmic opponent of God as defeated even before the battle has begun."[8] Finally, John 16:11 reiterates the coming judgment on Satan. Here Jesus reminds his disciples that the judgment on the world is directly related to the judgment on Satan. Because Satan is judged, those whom he rules over will also be judged.

Satan's Minions

Satan does not work alone but appears to be the leader of lesser evil spirits. In the Gospels, the devil is called the "prince [or "ruler," *archōn*]

---

8   Edward W. Klink III, *John*, ZECNT (Grand Rapids, MI: Zondervan, 2016), 642.

of demons" (Matt. 9:34; 12:24; Mark 3:22; Luke 11:15). Several times in Ephesians Paul references spiritual forces using various terms:

- "rulers," *archai* (1:21; 3:10; 6:12)[9]
- "authorities," *exousiai* (1:21; 2:2; 3:10; 6:12)[10]
- "powers," *dynameis* (1:21)[11]
- "dominions," *kyriotētes* (1:21)[12]
- "cosmic powers," *kosmokratores* (6:12)
- "the spiritual forces of evil" (6:12)

In his first prayer, Paul mentions the mighty power that raised Jesus from the dead and "seated him at his right hand in the heavenly places, far above all rule and authority and power and dominion, and above every name that is named, not only in this age but also in the one to come" (1:20–21). Although the four terms that Paul uses might have distinct nuances, the point that Paul is making is that Jesus has supremacy over all other beings. In fact, Jesus is exalted "above every name that is named" (1:21; cf. Phil. 2:9–10). This global reference demonstrates that Paul did not intend to exhaust all the names. The calling of the names of supernatural powers was common in the magic practices in Ephesus (cf. Eph. 3:15). Arnold notes, "Supernatural 'powers' were called upon by name . . . by one who desired access to their powers and assistance."[13] Paul emphasizes the reign and sovereignty of Christ over all powers, not only in this age but also in the age to come.

In chapter 3 Paul declares that grace was given to him to preach Christ to the Gentiles and to reveal the once-hidden mystery "so that through the church the manifold wisdom of God might now be made known to the rulers and authorities in the heavenly places" (3:10). Thus by its very existence, the church (made up of Jews and Gentiles in one

---

9 See also Rom. 8:38; 1 Cor. 15:24; Col. 1:16; 2:15.
10 See also Col. 1:16; 2:15; 1 Pet. 3:22.
11 See also Rom. 8:38; 1 Cor. 15:24; 1 Pet. 3:22.
12 See also Col. 1:16.
13 Arnold, *Power and Magic*, 54.

body) proclaims the wisdom of God as a testimony to these spiritual powers. Arnold interprets, "The existence of the church thereby demonstrates to the 'powers' that they are in fact powerless to impede the progress of the gospel to the Gentiles and consequently destroy the church, the body of Christ, which they thought they had already once destroyed on the cross."[14] The "rulers and authorities" are therefore hostile spiritual powers that cannot ultimately thwart God's purposes through his people.

Finally, Paul concludes his letter with a call to wage war against an invisible enemy. He writes, "For we do not wrestle against flesh and blood, but against the rulers, against the authorities, against the cosmic powers over this present darkness, against the spiritual forces of evil in the heavenly places" (6:12). The first two categories (rulers and authorities) overlap with those found in 1:21 but the last two are unique to the New Testament. Although these four designations are sometimes viewed as four distinct rankings or as portraying a hierarchical structure among the devil's inimical cohort, such a view is difficult to maintain since the relationship between these powers and the devil is never delineated. Additionally, nearly every list of these (and other) terms has a different combination of the terms.[15] Consequently, any attempt to classify various groupings of evil spirits is difficult and goes beyond the information provided in Scripture. We can be certain, however, that these terms represent personal, demonic beings (and are not merely impersonal social forces), and that these evil spirits are determined to cause harm to God's people.

Satan's Power and Influence

Although Satan is not all-powerful, he does possess power and is able to influence people. Prior to receiving salvation and transferring kingdom alliances, believers are characterized as being spiritually dead, as those who once walked according to the "course [or "age," *aiōn*] of

---

14 Arnold, *Power and Magic*, 64.
15 See Eph. 1:21; 3:10; 6:12. Also see Rom. 8:38; 1 Cor. 15:24; Col. 1:16; 1 Pet. 3:22.

this world" (2:1–2). Satan is not idle but is "now at work in the sons of disobedience" (2:2). The devil is working his evil plan to destroy humanity, or, as Peter states, he "prowls around like a roaring lion, seeking someone to devour" (1 Pet. 5:8). In Ephesians 4, Paul warns believers not to let their anger fester ("do not let the sun go down on your anger," 4:26) because in doing so, they may give an "opportunity to the devil" (4:27). Paul's fear is that unchecked anger can be exploited by the devil, which will lead to further sin. Believers must be cautious and not give the devil a chance to exert his influence at times when they are susceptible, especially when the unity of the church is at stake.

The epic battle between God's people and Satan and his demonic forces is most clearly spelled out in Ephesians 6. Christians are to arm themselves with the full or complete armor of God in order "to stand against the schemes of the devil" (6:11). The devil is actively planning and strategizing as to how to make God's people retreat or fall. Arnold suggests that such attacks "could come through people who teach things contrary to the 'one faith' (4:5), through temptation, difficult physical trials, or overt manifestations, or through any of a limitless array of intelligently designed plots."[16] Paul, therefore, calls on believers to "wrestle" against these hostile invisible foes (6:12). Part of the spiritual armor needed is the shield of faith, which "can extinguish all the flaming darts of the evil one" (6:16). With this defensive weapon (faith), believers can extinguish the flaming arrows (attacks) of the evil one (the devil). The word "darts" (*belos*) refers to "a missile, including arrows (propelled by a bow) or darts (hurled by hand)."[17] This could be an arrow, dart, spear, or javelin. That the darts are "flaming" indicates the hostile and destructive nature of Satan's attacks.

Elsewhere in the New Testament, we learn that Satan and his minions tempt believers in other ways. Married couples are encouraged not to deprive one another sexually but to abstain for only a limited time so that they are not tempted by Satan because of their lack of self-control

16 Clinton E. Arnold, *Ephesians*, ZECNT (Grand Rapids, MI: Zondervan, 2010), 445.
17 L&N 6.36.

(1 Cor. 7:5). A lack of forgiveness that leads to discord can be the result of being "outwitted by Satan," who plans or schemes to take down God's people (2 Cor. 2:10–11). Church leaders should have a good reputation so that they do not "fall into disgrace, into a snare of the devil" (1 Tim. 3:7). Younger widows should marry, have children, and manage their homes so that they "give the adversary no occasion for slander. For some have already strayed after Satan" (1 Tim. 5:14–15). Paul states that the Lord's servant should correct opponents with gentleness so that God may perhaps grant them repentance, which leads them to a knowledge of the truth (2 Tim. 2:24–25), "and they may come to their senses and escape from the snare of the devil, after being captured by him to do his will" (2 Tim. 2:26). These texts (and others) demonstrate that Satan and his cohorts are actively seeking to destroy believers through temptations and snares. In the end, believers need to trust in the goodness of God and his will for his people. As Paul states, "The Lord is faithful. He will establish you and guard you against the evil one" (2 Thess. 3:3).

The Present Reign of Christ

Christ's Lordship

In at least eight texts in Ephesians, Jesus is explicitly identified as Lord (1:2, 3, 15, 17; 3:11; 5:20; 6:23, 24) and is the referent in most of the eighteen other uses of the word in Ephesians. Although the term *lord* (*kurios*) can be used in various contexts to mean "sir" or "master/lord," when it is associated with Jesus, it is a reference to his supreme authority. Indeed, YHWH in the Old Testament is designated with this same title, and in several New Testament passages Paul applies the Old Testament text to Christ.[18] In the Greco-Roman context, deities were often given the title "Lord," an appellation that was also applied to emperors (in the late first century). Furthermore, in a location like Ephesus that placed a high value on magic and power, it is not surprising that Paul emphasizes the lordship of Jesus. Jesus is the sole and supreme Lord, and no malignant power is able to compete with his authority.

---

18 See, e.g., Rom. 10:13 (Joel 2:32); 1 Cor. 1:31 (Jer. 9:23–24); 10:26 (Ps. 24:1).

The lordship of Jesus is not only expressed in the designation "Lord," but it is also demonstrated through his designation as "head." More specifically, Jesus is named as "head" (*kephalē*) of the church. The church itself represents the culmination of God's plan to unite Jews and Gentiles into one body. And the one who leads the church is Christ. He is the head and Savior of the church (5:23). Christians are to mature in their faith and become like Christ, the head of the church (4:15). But Christ is not only head of the church; Paul declares that he is also head of creation (i.e., all things): God has "put all things under his feet and gave him as head over all things to the church, which is his body" (1:22–23).[19] Although "all things" should be understood universally, because Paul recently mentioned Christ's supremacy "far above all rule and authority and power and dominion" (1:21), Paul is highlighting his rule over powers and principalities. Similarly, in Colossians Paul writes that Christ "is the head of all rule and authority" (Col. 2:10). Thus Paul asserts the lordship of Christ via his reference to Christ being the head of the church and of all creation.

Christ's status as head is also revealed in God's plan "to unite all things in him, things in heaven and things on earth" (Eph. 1:10). The word translated "unite" (*anakephalaioō*) could be rendered "to bring under the headship of." Christ not only created all things (John 1:3; Col. 1:16; Heb. 1:2; Rev. 4:11), but all things will be consummated under his headship and through his power. "All things" refers to the entire universe ("things in heaven and things on earth"), including all evil spirits. The culmination of God's plan includes the summing up of all things, which involves the subjection of all things to Christ. God will unite the entire cosmos under Christ.

Christ's Kingdom

The present reign of Christ is further seen in his status as a king who rules a kingdom. Paul states that those who are sexually immoral, impure, or greedy have "no inheritance in the kingdom of Christ and

---

19   See also Col. 1:18; 2:10, 19.

God" (Eph. 5:5). Interestingly, Paul uses the phrase "kingdom of Christ" only here. Though debated by scholars, the two kingdoms ("kingdom of Christ" and "kingdom of God") probably should not be considered as distinct realities. In the Gospels, the kingdom of God was inaugurated in Jesus's life and ministry (especially his resurrection from the dead), and it will be consummated when he returns. In Ephesians, Paul emphasizes the present reign of Christ along with the present benefits of being united to him by faith. Christ is even now ruling with his enemies under his feet, and believers are seated with him in victory, given a new citizenship and membership into God's house (1:20–22; 2:6, 19). But there are also future benefits that await believers when they will enjoy the fullness of the kingdom. There is a future inheritance (1:13–14; 4:30; 5:5), a time when the warfare against inimical forces will be over. As King, Christ presently rules over his kingdom, which will one day be fully consummated, and which includes the defeat of all hostile enemies and even the defeat of death itself.

Although Paul does not often speak of the kingdom of Christ/God,[20] he does use language that describes actions that only kings do. For example, in his first prayer he describes the power of God as God raised Christ from the dead and "seated him at his right hand in the heavenly places" (1:20). This coronation language further emphasizes that Christ has unrivaled authority as the enthroned King who is Lord over all creation, including all principalities and powers. Paul's language echoes Psalm 110:1: "The Lord says to my Lord: 'Sit at my right hand, until I make your enemies your footstool.'" This enthronement psalm refers to a Davidic king who will ascend to the throne and reign in the position of highest honor. Christ's regal authority is also displayed in Ephesians 2:6 where Paul states that believers are raised with Christ and seated with Christ in the heavenly places. Because of their union with Christ, believers share in Christ's victory, authority, and kingdom.

---

20 Paul uses the term kingdom (basileia) only fourteen times: Rom. 14:17; 1 Cor. 4:20; 6:9, 10; 15:24, 50; Gal. 5:21; Eph. 5:5; Col. 1:13; 4:11; 1 Thess. 2:12; 2 Thess. 1:5; 2 Tim. 4:1, 18.

Christ's Gifts

As the Lord of heaven and earth, Christ is a benevolent King who loves his children and supplies them with every good and perfect gift. Paul refers to the "unsearchable riches of Christ" (3:8). The riches that Christ possesses cannot be searched out or calculated. Christ does not keep these riches for himself but lavishes them upon his followers. Indeed, he has blessed them now "with every spiritual blessing in the heavenly places" (1:3). But he also has promised them a future inheritance. This inheritance cannot be lost or forfeited, because Christ has sealed us with the Holy Spirit, "who is the guarantee of our inheritance until we acquire possession of it" (1:14), that is, until "the day of redemption" (4:30). And yet Paul warns that those who do not live a Spirit-filled and Spirit-empowered life—but live in immorality, impurity, or idolatry—have "no inheritance in the kingdom of Christ and God" (5:5).

As King, Christ also gives gifts to his church. Paul explains how the ascended conqueror blesses his church with gifts. After vanquishing his enemies (including the evil, spiritual forces), Christ ascended to his heavenly throne and now distributes divine gifts to each member of his body (4:7). Paul writes, quoting Psalm 68:18, "When he ascended on high he led a host of captives, and he gave gifts to men" (4:8). Not only does Christ endow his people with gifts, but his people are the gifts to the church: "And he gave the apostles, the prophets, the evangelists, the shepherds and teachers" (4:11). These leaders are given to build up the body of Christ (4:12). Therefore, Christ blesses his people with every spiritual blessing, a future inheritance, and spiritual gifts that include leaders for the church.

The Present Battle

The Christian's Struggle

Paul's epistle to the Ephesians makes clear that believers are engaged in a spiritual battle against a real enemy. In 6:11–12 Paul mentions (1) the devil, (2) rulers, (3) authorities, (4) cosmic powers, and (5) spiritual forces. But the spiritual nature of the enemy makes it necessary to be fitted with divinely supplied armor (more on this below). The imagery of armor signifies warfare. Paul states, "For we do not wrestle against flesh and blood" (6:12). The word translated "wrestle" (*palē*) occurs only here in the Bible and was typically used for the sport of wrestling. With the use of military imagery of armor and weaponry, however, Paul envisions a fierce battle and not merely an intense, but safe, athletic competition. The wrestling metaphor, however, does demonstrate the closeness of the battle. It is also a battle not fought against "flesh and blood" (i.e., humanity), but against powers and principalities. Earlier, Paul referenced how the Ephesian believers at one time were "darkness," but now they are "light in the Lord" (5:8). But the powers of darkness do not surrender when someone follows Christ. Instead, the cosmic battle intensifies, and the Christian is now the object of the devil's attacks.

The Christian's Strength

In light of the believer's struggle, Paul exhorts his readers to "be strong in the Lord and in the strength of his might" (6:10). The passive voice ("be strengthened") reminds us that the strength to fight against the attacks of Satan and his minions comes not from ourselves but from the Lord. Thus Paul both urges his readers to action and, at the same time, reminds them that the power comes from an external source. Earlier Paul prayed that his readers might "be strengthened with power through his Spirit in [their] inner being" (3:16). Similarly, Paul encourages Timothy, "You then, my child, be strengthened by the grace that is in Christ Jesus" (2 Tim. 2:1). The source of our power comes through our union with the Lord Jesus Christ. In the midst of intense spiritual warfare, the power to fight and to stand firm comes through a genuine relationship with the resurrected and ascended Christ. Satan and his minions are well-armed and can easily wound or discourage weary soldiers of the cross. The strength to fight and overcome the enemy is supplied by God. Only by "the strength of his might" can believers be in a position to take a stand against the devil. Believers need divine, supernatural strength that only a living, reigning King can supply in order to overcome the forces of evil.

The Christian's Stand

Because the enemy is real and the battle rages on, Paul states four times that believers need to take a stand (Eph. 6:11, 13 [2x], 14). Significantly, believers are not told to win the victory—the victory has already been secured by Christ. Instead, they are urged to stand firm against the onslaught of the spiritual forces that wage warfare against them. Standing firm conveys more than just not retreating. It also implies a forceful offensive against one's opponent. Arnold writes, "The struggle/warfare can best be described in terms of an offensive aspect (making the gospel known) and a defensive aspect (resisting temptation; endurance)."[21]

The way in which believers engage in this warfare and withstand the assault of the enemy is to put on "the whole armor [*panoplia*] of God" (6:11), which includes a belt, breastplate, shoes, shield, helmet, and sword. The emphasis is on the full protection that the armor supplies. The term *panoplia* indicates the full set of armor that a Roman foot soldier would wear into battle, though not every piece of the armor is listed. But it would be a mistake to limit the background of Paul's metaphor to the Roman soldier. Rather, Paul draws imagery from Isaiah that depicts Yahweh and his Messiah as the divine warrior who is clothed with armor as he prepares for battle to defend and vindicate his people (Isa. 11:4–5; 52:7; 59:17).[22]

Paul lists six pieces of armor that believers need in order to be equipped to stand firm. The first piece of armor is "the belt of truth" (Eph. 6:14). The verb translated "having fastened" literally means to "gird or prepare oneself" and indicates preparation for action. In this context, it signifies readiness to engage in battle. Paul seems to draw imagery from Isaiah 11:5: "He shall be girded with righteousness around his waist, and bound with truth around the sides" (NETS). The armor worn by the righteous and truthful Messiah is now given to his people in order that they might stand firm in the midst of spiritual warfare. The belt is described (and thus equated) with truth. That is, Christians

---

21 Arnold, *Power and Magic*, 121.

22 Paul also uses war or fighting imagery in several other passages (see Rom. 13:12; 2 Cor. 6:7; 10:3–6; 1 Thess. 5:8; 1 Tim. 1:18; 2 Tim. 2:3–4).

will be strengthened by the truth of God revealed in the gospel, and by doing so they will display the attributes of the Messiah in their attitudes and actions.

The second piece of armor is "the breastplate of righteousness" (Eph. 6:14). The "breastplate" (*thōrax*) was "a piece of armor covering the chest to protect it against blows and arrows."[23] Again, the language here is reminiscent of Isaiah 59:17 where Yahweh "put on righteousness as a breastplate." Here in Ephesians 6:14, righteousness does not refer to God's justifying, forensic righteousness, but is an ethical quality of doing what is right (see 4:24; 5:9). Christians are thus protected from the enemy by righteousness; that is, by imitating the righteous character of God himself.

The third piece of armor is "shoes for your feet" (6:15), which represent "the readiness given by the gospel of peace." Isaiah 52:7 reads, "How beautiful upon the mountains are the feet of him who brings good news, who publishes peace." Only those who have their feet properly fitted will be equipped and prepared for spiritual warfare. The meaning here could refer either to the preparation that comes from the gospel or readiness to proclaim the gospel. The former option means that believers are prepared for spiritual warfare and able to stand firm through the powerful message of the gospel, which is a message of peace (a defensive posture). The latter option involves the willingness of the believer to announce the good news about Jesus Christ and the peace he brings through reconciling God and man (an offensive posture). If Isaiah 52:7 is seen as the source of Paul's imagery, then the latter is to be preferred.[24]

The fourth piece of armor is "the shield of faith" (Eph. 6:16). The large shield carried by Roman soldiers could protect a soldier's entire body. When soaked in water, these shields could extinguish arrows that were dipped in pitch and set on fire before they were shot. In the Old Testament, the imagery of a shield often represented God's protection

---

23 L&N 6.39.

24 Also, the "sword of the Spirit" (6:17) that represents the word of God is an offensive weapon. In addition, compare the way in which Paul asks for prayer that he might boldly preach the gospel (6:19–20).

of his people (see Gen. 15:1). Believers are shielded from the enemy by their faith, confidence, and trust in God. Lincoln comments, "Faith takes hold of God's resources in the midst of the onslaughts of evil and produces the firm resolve which douses anything the enemy throws at the believer."[25]

The fifth piece of armor is "the helmet of salvation" (Eph. 6:17). Paul's language here again echoes Isaiah 59 where Yahweh put on "a helmet of salvation" (Isa. 59:17). Paul does not exhort his readers to embrace salvation since they already possess it. Rather, they must constantly appropriate it by faith. Thus to put on salvation "means to realize and appropriate one's new identity in Christ, which gives believers power for deliverance from the supernatural enemies on the basis of their union with the resurrected and exalted Lord."[26]

The final piece of armor or weaponry is "the sword of the Spirit" (Eph. 6:17). This particular sword (*machaira*) is "a relatively short sword (or even dagger) used for cutting and stabbing" designed for close combat.[27] The sword is related to the Spirit because the Spirit is what makes the sword powerful and effective. This Spirit-given sword is not a physical sword but is "the word [*rhema*] of God," i.e., the gospel. This offensive weapon is the good news of peace and reconciliation that believers both embrace and proclaim. The result of faithfully using the armor of God is that believers will be able to stand firm against hostile, spiritual enemies.

Although Paul does not include prayer as an additional piece of armor, it is intimately related to spiritual warfare. He writes:

> ... praying at all times in the Spirit, with all prayer and supplication. To that end, keep alert with all perseverance, making supplication for all the saints, and also for me, that words may be given to me in opening my mouth boldly to proclaim the mystery of the gospel, for which I am an ambassador in chains, that I may declare it boldly, as I ought to speak. (6:18–20)

25 Andrew D. Lincoln, *Ephesians*, WBC 42 (Dallas: Word, 1990), 449.

26 Arnold, *Ephesians*, 460.

27 L&N 6.33.

Prayer is the means by which believers stand firm and equip themselves with the whole armor of God. Without prayer, the armor and weapons needed for battle will not be effectively employed. As such, prayer plays a foundational role for the effective deployment of all the armor and weapons, and epitomizes what it means to be strong in the Lord (6:10).

The divine source of power is highlighted in this passage as Paul indicates all three persons of the Trinity in relation to this spiritual battle: God the Father is the divine warrior who makes his armor and weaponry available to his people. It is the complete armor "of God" (6:11, 13). Additionally, believers are told to take up the "word of God" (6:17). God the Son, who is now the exalted Lord seated at the Father's right hand, is the one who strengthens believers who are to "be strong in the Lord" (6:10). God the Spirit likewise provides the Christian soldier with the sword since it comes from the Spirit (6:17). Furthermore, believers are also instructed to pray "in the Spirit" (6:18).

The Present Age and the Age to Come

Paul's theology includes two ages: (1) the current age, which is characterized by spiritual warfare against wicked powers, and (2) the coming age, which will be characterized by peace and righteousness in the presence of God. But this twofold schema is complicated by at least two factors. First, sometimes Paul speaks, not in terms of God's universal plan in light of the big picture, but in terms of an individual's or a group's salvation experience. Second, there is an overlap of the ages where some of the benefits that will belong to believers in the future are proleptically experienced now. That is, some of the blessings of the age to come are currently enjoyed by God's people. The consummation of the kingdom will occur when all things are united in Christ.

"Once" vs. "But Now"

Several times in Ephesians Paul contrasts the situation of believers before their conversion with their current situation as followers of Christ. Before they were spiritually awakened by the power of God, they were dead in their sins in which they "once [*pote*] walked," following the world, the flesh, and the devil (2:2). Indeed, "we all once [*pote*] lived" as those who were disobedient. Our pre-Christian experience was characterized by fulfilling the desires of the flesh. Often, Paul contrasts the former (*pote*) way of life with the current ("now," *nun*) situation (see 2:11, 13; 5:8). In this passage, however, the "now" is implied (2:4–10). Formerly, believers walked as the living dead, following their sinful passions. "But God" had mercy on them and changed the course of their lives.

Later in chapter 2, Paul again uses the "once/formerly" (*pote*), "but now" (*nun de*) contrast. He urges his non-Jewish readers to "remember that at one time [*pote*] you Gentiles in the flesh . . . were at that time separated from Christ, alienated from the commonwealth of Israel and strangers to the covenants of promise, having no hope and without God in the world" (2:11–12). These verses highlight the former predicament of Gentiles by using both "at one time" (*pote*) and "at that time." The dramatic change in the status of Gentile believers is then emphasized by the words "but now." Paul continues, "But now [*nuni de*] in Christ Jesus you who once were far off have been brought near by the blood of Christ" (2:13). He later adds, "So then you are no longer [*ouketi*] strangers and aliens, but you are fellow citizens with the saints and members of the household of God" (2:19). Once again Paul contrasts the preconverted past of those who were far from God with the miraculous change and current situation of those who are now near to God and part of his covenant family.

Finally, in chapter 5, we see this same pattern emerge as Paul uses the contrasting imagery of darkness and light: "For at one time [*pote*] you were darkness, but now [*nun de*] you are light in the Lord. Walk as children of light" (5:8). The personal transformation from darkness to light, from being dead in sins to being made alive by the power of God, from being strangers and aliens to citizens and household members, is repeatedly emphasized by Paul in Ephesians.[28] But Paul also has in

---

28 For this same (or similar) pattern elsewhere in Paul, see Rom. 11:30 (*pote . . . nuni de*); Col. 1:21–22 (*pote . . . nuni de*); 3:7–8 (*pote . . . nuni de*); Titus 3:3–4 (*pote . . . hote de*).

mind another contrast that is bigger in scale, not simply involving an individual's destiny, but revolving around the inauguration of God's kingdom along with its impending consummation.

Already vs. Not Yet

In his first coming, Jesus ushered in the kingdom of God. It is already here. It arrived when King Jesus arrived, especially in his resurrection and ascension. And yet the kingdom is still future. Because sin and death remain, we still wait for the fullness of the kingdom to be consummated at Christ's second coming. This type of *inaugurated eschatology* is consistent with Paul's vision of the present and future found in Ephesians. Although it is true that Ephesians often stresses the present benefits of being in Christ (a realized eschatology), at times we also see an occasional focus on the hope of a new age to come (future eschatology). For example, in his first prayer, Paul states that Christ is not only given a position "far above all rule and authority and power and dominion," but he is given that position "not only in this age but also in the one to come" (1:21). Here Paul delineates two ages, "this age" and "the one to come." Matthew records a saying of Jesus that contains the same phrases: "And whoever speaks a word against the Son of Man will be forgiven, but whoever speaks against the Holy Spirit will not be forgiven, either in this age or in the age to come" (Matt. 12:32). "This age" spans between the first and second advent of Christ, and "the age to come" begins at the return of Christ when the kingdom arrives in its fullness.

What does "this age" consist of? On the one hand, because of the work of Christ in securing salvation for his people, for believers this age means receiving "every spiritual blessing in the heavenly places" (Eph. 1:3). They are chosen, redeemed, forgiven, and sealed with the Spirit (1:3–14). But in the same passage they are also promised an inheritance, which by definition is something that is still future (1:11–12). The mystery ("that the Gentiles are fellow heirs, members of the same body, and partakers of the promise in Christ Jesus through the gospel," 3:6) that was hidden in other generations "has now been revealed to his holy apostles and prophets by the Spirit" (3:5). Through his apostles and prophets, in this age God has revealed to us his plan in the gospel of Jesus Christ to create one new humanity, the church.

But believers still long for "the age to come." We have been sealed with the Holy Spirit "for the day of redemption" (4:30). So even though we have already been redeemed (1:7; Col. 1:14), we still await a future redemption, including "the redemption of our bodies" (Rom. 8:23). Because evil and darkness still pervade our world, our ultimate redemption has not been achieved (though it has been secured). Paul encourages us to make "the best use of the time, because the days are evil" (Eph. 5:16). Again, Paul's language reflects an eschatological perspective. The world in which we now live will not endure forever because the stain of sin and evil still mar it (Rom. 8:18–22). Best comments, "If some days are described as evil this must imply there are 'good' days; since these are not now they must lie in the future."[29] Paul later urges Christians to employ the full armor of God so that they "may be able to withstand in the evil day" (Eph. 6:13). Similarly, in Galatians 1:4 he states that Christ died to deliver his people "from the present evil age." The interadvental age can be characterized as an "evil age" because evil often goes unchecked and seems to flourish. God's people should not be discouraged or disillusioned, however. During this present age God's Spirit inhabits his people, and he will never leave them or forsake them. Christ's work is finished, and the kingdom will one day be consummated.

The Consummation of All Things

I began this book by discussing God's plan to unite all things in Christ, focusing on Ephesians 1:10. I will now conclude by returning to this theme. To review, we noted that God's plan to "unite all things in Christ" includes the following: (1) In his abundant grace, God *reveals* his plan to his people. (2) This plan is the revealing of a *mystery* that Gentiles would be considered equal with Israel. (3) This plan was revealed by

---

29 E. Best, *Ephesians*, ICC (London: T&T Clark, 1998), 504.

God according to his *purpose* or *good pleasure*, which demonstrates that God delights in redeeming lost sinners. (4) God set forth his plan *in Christ* who was intimately involved in planning our redemption with the Father. (5) God set forth this plan in *the fullness of time*, which means that the life, death, resurrection, and ascension of Jesus are the pivotal acts in redemptive history. (6) God's plan is *to unite all things* through Christ, which includes not just all humanity but also the angelic realm, both good and evil, and the entire cosmos. (7) This plan *centers on Christ* since he is not only the means by which God will unite all the disparate elements of creation together, but he is the center and focal point through whom and for whom all this will take place.

The last days in which we live will one day end, and God's people will enjoy the new heavens and the new earth. Every person will face judgment, but those who are in Christ will be "holy and blameless before him" (1:4). At that time, God's enemies will be vanquished, and Christ will deliver "the kingdom to God the Father after destroying every rule and every authority and power" (1 Cor. 15:24). Until then we wait, and we persevere in the strength that God provides (1 Pet. 4:11).

The God of peace will soon crush Satan under your feet. (Rom. 16:20)

General Index

Scripture Index

The New Testament Theology Series

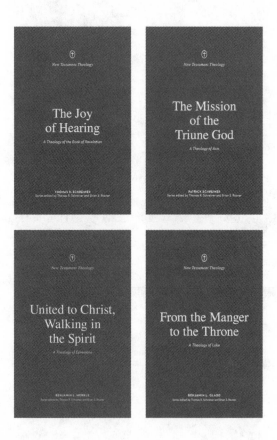

Edited by Thomas R. Schreiner and Brian S. Rosner, this series presents clear, scholarly overviews of the main theological themes of each book of the New Testament, examining what they reveal about God, Christ, and how they connect to the overarching biblical narrative.

For more information, visit **crossway.org**.